RIOT IN HEAVEN
(voices of color speak!)

Second Edition

Osonye Tess Onwueme

RIOT IN HEAVEN

a play

by

Osonye Tess Onwueme

AFRICAN HERITAGE PRESS
NEW YORK · LAGOS · LONDON
2006

AFRICAN HERITAGE PRESS

NEW YORK	LAGOS
PO BOX 1433	PO BOX 14452
NEW ROCHELLE	IKEJA, LAGOS
NY 10802, USA	NIGERIA

TEL: 718-862-3262
FAX: 718-862-1440
EMAIL: afroheritage9760@aol.com
www.africanheritagepress.com

First Edition, Africana Legacy Press, 1997

Copyright © Onwueme Tess, 2006

Library of Congress catalog number: 2006937452
Onwueme Tess

Distributors: African Books Collective,
                 www.africanbookscollective.com

African Heritage Press is an affiliate of African Books Collective,
(ABC), PO Box 721, Oxford, OX1 9EN, UK.
Tel/Fax +44 (0) 1869 34110, orders@africanbookscollective.com

Cover Design: **African Heritage Press**

Selections: 2006

Drama, African Drama, African Literature, Gender Studies, Ethnic
Studies, Multicultural Studies, African American Literature.

ISBN: 978-0-9790858-0-2
ISBN: 0-9790858-0-2

DEDICATION

for

Mama Regina
Nwa Odiwé
oka onwéné
Afàà Nnem!

Chim!
Chi onye éduè!
Afàà Nnem

ACKNOWLEDGMENTS

Sharon Bejin's passion for learning and painstaking attention to detail facilitated the realization of this final product. Her invaluable enterprise in helping to edit this edition of the play will remain ever cherished.

And to my publisher African Heritage Press and our dear friend Mike Anibogu whose tireless devotion, faith, and commitment sustain the creative lives of many like me, I pray for God's guidance and relentless reward.

OTHER BOOKS BY THE AUTHOR

Comments by Scholars on Onwueme's Writings

Riot [in Heaven] is an excellent and spectacular piece of drama. The language, imagery, allegories, symbols, songs, music and dance come together like a complex jigsaw puzzle. Onwueme's use of music, especially the Negro Spirituals carefully inserted at strategic moments in the play, is perceptive and powerfully evocative. It seems Onwueme packs her whole creative self into this work and excels herself ideologically, structurally, aesthetically and politically.

Dr. Omofalabo Ajayi, *African Theatre: Women.*
Indiana University Press, 2002.

The protagonists of Dr. Tess Onwueme's plays tend to be women who revolt against their misuse by an outdated and inhumane system... In many ways, one might see Tess Onwueme as the 'Ibsen' of her culture; the playwright who dares to raise new issues and write 'A Doll's House' so to speak for her people... These sociological reasons allow us North Americans to identify strongly with the women in Tess Onwueme's plays. Her dramas are very much universal plays for an international audience as they speak to us of basic human rights of nationality, age, sex, or race.

Professor Daniella Gioseffi, winner
1990 National Book Award.

Tess Akaeke Onwueme is not a radical feminist, but in all her plays, she devotes considerable attention to feminist themes... Like many good writers, she is an idealist, and it is this idealism that attracts her creative sensibility to the potential of mythology. Placed at the service of her feminist interests, the mythical lends itself to an art, which rises above the banality of mere ideological proselytizing. She takes a careful look at traditional African (Igbo) institutions and sees in them authentic materials, which though often institutionalized by retrogressive patriarchy over the years, can be put to good use for the cause of positive change. She is an artist who deliberately throws stones into ponds in order to cause ripples.

Dr. Afam Ebeogu,
The Literary Griot: International Journal of Black Oral & Literary Studies, 3, 1 (Spring 1991), 109.

CAST: Travelers On The Crossroads

TRAVELER-X: A middle-aged man of African descent at the crossroads and caught in the dilemma of border crossing and transitioning through passages. With each passage he is transformed, changing from being GARVEY, MANDELA, and the FATHER/GRIOT in his other lives to losing it all and becoming "X" in his present struggle at the crossroads. In the play, he is either THE TRAVELER or TRAVELER-X.

THE MOTHER/SOUJOURNER NKRUMAH: A 35-year old woman of African descent. Ragged and almost half-naked, she has a stuffed baby doll strapped on her back, always. Like TRAVELER-X, she has been through many transitions as BABE, SOJOURNER NKRUMAH, until becoming THE MOTHER in the Dream Sequence of the drama.

STANLEY LIVINGSTONE: One of the self-appointed keepers of Heavensgate. He is a powerful representative of the church and the Euro-American world.

JEFFERSON LUGARD: Lord of the Empire and co-keeper of Heavensgate.

LADY JEFFERSON LUGARD: Lady of the Empire. Wife of LORD JEFFERSON LUGARD. She has a habit of hanging her bra and underwear in front of Heavensgate.

JAH ORISHA: The ancient voice of wisdom or God.

THE UNSEEN: Communal voices, initially led by JAH ORISHA. They are the ever-present Living and Dead people of African descent who keep coming and going, with their "drum voices" resonating in chants.

THE FATHER/GRIOT: In the first passage, he is the GRIOT/X. As GRIOT he is the people's historian/preacher until he finally attains rebirth and becomes THE FATHER in the Dream Sequence of the drama. In his other incarnations and passages, he is the TRAVELER-X.

THE SETTING

Armed with his trumpet, TRAVELER-X, a man of African descent is at the crossroads of Earth, Heaven and Hell. Each road has its own route/exit. Hell is Zero Exit. Earth is Route XYZ with the inscription: "Promises no safety. Proceed at your own risk." Heaven is the right barricaded winding road, marked "Route 739-436-3689." The barricade at Heavensgate reads, "Aliens crossing: Watch Out!" Of all the exits, Hell is where the music is. It's where the action is. The black woman acts as the disc jockey and gatekeeper of Hell where she compels all with her life-song: The Soul-Train which she sings at crucial moments in their passage:

> *Soul train, it's where the action is.*
> *Hell is fine music.*
> *No hurry! No worry! No ticket!*
> *Free parking! Free visa! Free passport!*
> *Free! Free! Free!*
> *Your freedom is our priority!*
> *Just come! Hell is fine music!*
> *It's where the action is!*

On the left side of the barricade at Heavensgate is the stalled Freedom Train or the Freedom Wagon. The Freedom Wagon belongs to SOJOURNER NKRUMAH, a middle-aged woman of African descent. Agonizing over the broken-down vehicle and constantly adjusting the stuffed baby doll on her back, the black woman struggles to polish and push her Freedom Train to her ultimate destination, Heaven. She realizes her quest only through solidarity with her estranged kinsman, TRAVELER-X.

THE STORY

Each struggling to enter Heaven, alone, the black man and black woman finally find each other and agree that their race has already paid enough dues. They scheme for TRAVELER-X to get into Heaven at all costs so that their people, too, will begin to have a voice and representation among the tribal saints of heaven. In the struggle, they realize that Heaven is too far, and that the paths are too narrow and thorny with many obstacles to their entry into this mythical heaven. The highest obstacles are imposed by two important historical figures: JEFFERSON LUGARD and STANLEY LIVINGSTONE, both heroes of the blessed history of the West. They are the self-appointed gatekeepers who have dethroned God and now reign in his place. Their alibi is that God has retired to go on vacation with Peter in a faraway land. Therefore, to protect Heaven against terrorists and the surging colored immigrants, God has left the key to heaven in the hands of JEFFERSON LUGARD and STANLEY LIVINGSTONE to enforce absolute security and ensure that only the chosen will be allowed to enter the gates of heaven. Neither SOJOURNER NKRUMAH nor TRAVELER-X is from the powerful ruling tribe of the JEFFERSON LUGARDS. These colored people are, therefore, barred from Heavensgate, in spite of their incessant struggle to make this passage. The banished aspirants question why they should be excluded from the rights and rites of passage into heaven, which the privileged tribe enjoys. But the gatekeepers remain adamant, demanding total expulsion of the unwelcome guests, lest these people of color also pollute heaven as they did Harlem, Brixton, Lagos, LA, and other cities. The conflict intensifies as both TRAVELER-X and SOJOURNER NKRUMAH scheme to break through the barrier and crash into Heaven. With SOJOURNER NKRUMAH's "Freedom Train" at a standstill, how then will these people of color get the key to open the passage to heaven for their own race? This sparks the Riot In Heaven.

FIRST PASSAGE: At the Border

(The stage blasts open with a song. At the center of it all is the stalled "Freedom Train." In spite of the militant vehicle's demobilized state, SOJOURNER NKRUMAH leans on it, strokes it and guards it jealously. Light flashes briefly on her as she sings and dances in her place with THE UNSEEN who have congregated as if in a Shrine or Black Church at the center of the crossroads. Accompanied by drums and percussions is the song, "JAH Sees Politricks: And History's Art, Not a Fact." THE UNSEEN chant in a call-response pattern.)

THE UNSEEN: History! History! His-tory! History's art, not a fact. History's art, not a fact!

SOLO: Politics-Politricks-Politricks!

CHORUS: History! History! His-tory-History's art, not a fact.

SOLO: JAH sees-

CHORUS: Sees-Sees-Sees!! Seas-Seas-Seas!!!

SOLO: Jah sees Po-lice-Politics-Politricks.

CHORUS: *(Echo.)* Politricks-Politricks-Politricks. Jah sees Politricks.

SOLO: And Politics?

CHORUS: Ha-Haaaa-Haaaaaaaaaaa!

SOLO: You got to learn?

CHORUS: *(Heightened music and dance.)* Learn! Learn! Learn. History! History's HER-STORY. History! History! His-tory! History's art, not a fact.

SOLO: You got to watch?

CHORUS: Watch! Watch! Watch!

SOLO: You got to count?

CHORUS: Count, count, count your vote! Count, count, count your vote!

1

SOLO: You got to write?

CHORUS: Write! Write! Write! History! History's Her-story! History's art, not a fact. History's art, not a fact.

SOLO: Oh, Jah sees-seas!

CHORUS: *(Echo.)* Jah Sees-Sees-Sees! Seas-Seas-Seas! *(Voices dying.)* History's art, not a fact.

THE FATHER/GRIOT/X: *(Enters, wearing the mask of MARCUS GARVEY like a high priest at the altar. He rouses the voices to action.)* Give it up Brethren!

THE UNSEEN: *(Loud applause.)* Amen!

THE FATHER/GRIOT/X: Give it up for JAH!

THE UNSEEN: Amen!

THE FATHER/GRIOT/X: Brothers 'n Sistus, I say give it up!

THE UNSEEN: Amen!

THE FATHER/GRIOT/X: Jah sees-sees-seas!

THE UNSEEN: Oh yes, Sees! Sees! Seas! Seas in me eyes!!

GRIOT/PREACHER: So give it up Brothers 'n Sistus! Give it up to Jeeee!

THE UNSEEN: *(Incantatory chant, ritual possession.)* God is good. Jah saves! Saves! Saves his own! Oh yeah! *(Speaking in tongues.)* Jah Saves! Save-Save-Save. JAH-JAH-JAH-JAH!

THE FATHER/GRIOT/X: And we say Amen?

THE UNSEEN: Amen to JAH!

THE FATHER/GRIOT/X: We say Amen?

THE UNSEEN: Amen! Amen! AMEEEEEEEEEEN!!! *(The song, "Sometimes I Feel Like a Motherless Child" swells in the background followed by a frenzied dance.)*

    SONG: SOMETIMES I FEEL LIKE A MOTHERLESS CHILD

Sometimes I feel like a motherless child
Sometimes I feel like a motherless child
Sometimes I feel like a motherless child
A long ways from home

2

A long ways from home
    True believer
    A long ways from home
    A long ways from home
Sometimes I feel like I'm almos gone,
Sometimes I feel like I'm almos gone,
Sometimes I feel like I'm almos gone,
Way up in de heab'nly lan'
Way up in de heab'nly lan'

True believer
A long ways from home
A long ways from home
Sometimes I feel like a motherless child
Sometimes I feel like a motherless child
Sometimes I feel like a motherless child
A long ways from home.

(Wailing chant intensifies and finally mellows down.)

SECOND PASSAGE: Crossing Borders (Drum Rituals/Showers)

(THE FATHER/GRIOT/X in another passage. He wears a different mask. This time in the image of MALCOLM X. Again, he has another encounter with THE UNSEEN voices that remain ever present.)

THE FATHER/GRIOT/X: When African drums turn talkative, who can silence the drums?

THE UNSEEN: *(Echo.)* Silences-Silences-Silences! Drum! Drum! Drum! Who can silence the drums?

THE FATHER/GRIOT/X: Five hundred seasons, the drums have been angry. Their voices inflamed, choking. Choking with tears from seasons of strife and whippings by the powers. How long must the drums be forced into silence? How long? How long? How long?

THE UNSEEN: *(Echo.)* Silences-Silences-Silences! Drum! Drum! Drum! Silences-Silences-Silences! Drum! Drum! Drum!

THE FATHER/GRIOT/X: The roads are burning!

THE UNSEEN: *(Wailing.)* Burning-Burning-Burning!

THE FATHER/GRIOT/X: The roads are thirsty!

THE UNSEEN: Thirsty-Thirsty-Thirsty!

THE FATHER/GRIOT/X: *(Calling.)* Drum Showers!

THE UNSEEN: *(Drums descending.)* Drum! Drum! Drum! Drum! Drum! Drum! Drum! Drum!

THE FATHER/GRIOT/X: Make way for the drums of passage!

THE UNSEEN: Make way, Make way! Make way for the drums of passage. Let the drums pass!

THE FATHER/GRIOT/X: Let the drums speak!

THE UNSEEN: *(Frenzied, speaking in tongues – Combination of African, Caribbean, Creole, Patoi and other transmutations and hybridization of African/European languag-*

es.) Duum! Duum! Duum! - Duum-Duum-Duum-Duum! - Dum! Dum! Dum! *(Sounds repeated until they drop into a murmur as THE FATHER/GRIOT/X proceeds.)*

THE FATHER/GRIOT/X: When the drums turn talkative, who can silence the drums? Drums, Drums, Drums will riot! Black drums turn talkative at the crossroads, as the *STANLEY LIVINGSTONES* and the *JEFFERSON LUGARDS* of the blessed history of the West, stand as twin-*Gods-Uke-Eshu: Legba-Elegbara-Ozebaa*. New Gods of passage at the crossroads? Wielding the keys of power at Heavensgate? And others locked out of Heavensgate? Why?

THE UNSEEN: *(Echoes.)* Why! Why! Why!

THE FATHER/GRIOT/X: They say Jah has gone on vacation with Peter. Jah left the seat of power to colorless Gods.

THE UNSEEN: Jah left the seat of power? How? How? How? How could our Savior leave the seat of power to hot-tempered Gods?

THE FATHER/GRIOT/X: Is God colorblind?

THE UNSEEN: Hmmm... No! Jah sees seas! Seas! Sees all. Except the minority. Jah is a minority here.

THE FATHER/GRIOT/X: Jah, a minority?

THE UNSEEN: *(Chanting.)* Yes, a minor-minority-minority God! Jah is a minority here!

THE FATHER/GRIOT/X: And this Traveler?

THE UNSEEN: *(Mock laughter.)* Ha! Ha! That man of color! Colorful! Color-fool-Duum! Color! Colorful! Color-fool-Dum! Duum! Drum! Duum! Drum! Duum! Drum!

THE FATHER/GRIOT/X: How can one of color break the jinx of power at Heavensgate?

THE UNSEEN: *(Chanting.)* How can? How can? How Can? How can the colorful break this jinx of color?

THE FATHER/GRIOT/X: For the race!

THE UNSEEN: Race-Race-Racists!

6

THE FATHER/GRIOT/X: Race tensions!

THE UNSEEN: *(Possessed, speaking in tongues.)* In LA! Jamestown! North Korea! New York! Baghdad! Brixton! Johannesburg! Palestine! Hutus and Tutsis! Liberia and Nigeria! Race! Run! Race...? *(Thunderclap.)*

THE FATHER/GRIOT/X: Tensions!

THE UNSEEN: *(Rolling thunder.)* Tensions-Tensions-Tensions!

THE FATHER/GRIOT/X: Rising?

THE UNSEEN: Rising! Rising! Rising to swell the mouth of the drums! Duum-Duum-Duum!! Drum showers! Drum! Drum! Drum! Talkative at crossroads!

THE FATHER/GRIOT/X: Drums turned to flames.

THE UNSEEN: *(Intoning.)* Hear! Voices! Voices! Voices of drums!

THE FATHER/GRIOT/X: Who can silence the drums?

THE UNSEEN: Who can silence the drums?

THE FATHER/GRIOT/X: Burning?

THE UNSEEN: *(Echo.)* Burning! Burning! Burning! Burning in Heaven.

THE FATHER/GRIOT/X: Voices!

THE UNSEEN: *(Rolling Thunder.)* Voices-voices-voices!

THE FATHER/GRIOT/X: Of color? Oh! Oh! Color burning! Voices burning! Burning in Heaven!

THE UNSEEN: *(Echo.)* Auu! Auu! Auu!

THE FATHER/GRIOT/X: Auu! Auu! Auu!

THE UNSEEN: *(Echo.)* Oh! Voices! Voices! Voices of color! *(Trumpets sound a brief reminder of "Sometimes I Feel Like a Motherless Child." THE UNSEEN hum, sing and dance along.)*

THE FATHER/GRIOT/X: Will the child of color... Will...?

THE UNSEEN: Will! Will the child of color will?

THE FATHER/GRIOT/X: Will the will to Heaven!

THE UNSEEN: Will-will-will! Will the child of color will the will to Heaven?

THE FATHER/GRIOT/X: That is the question! Will the child of color will the will to Heaven?

THE UNSEEN: *(Echo.)* The Question–Question–Question!

THE FATHER/GRIOT/X: The Question! Question! Question! Question as riot!

THE UNSEEN: Riot in Heaven! *(Darkness descends. Violent drum sounds and deafening gunshots suddenly pierce through, disrupting and scattering the crowd now scouting for cover. Then silence. In one corner, the shrill sound of a mother's wailing is heard. The crowd gathers again, sad, subdued but still defiant. As they gather, they join hands and start lifting their fallen hero. THE FATHER/GRIOT/X is the victim of the violent encounter. Slowly, THE UNSEEN converge in a circle as they lift up THE FATHER/GRIOT/X sky-high, humming a tune, until they break into a clarion call of "Go Down Moses.")*

THE UNSEEN:

Go Down Moses
Way down in Egypt land.
Tell ole-Pharaoh,
To let my people go.

> *Go down Moses*
> *Way down in Egypt land.*
> *Tell ole-Pharaoh,*
> *To let my people go.*

When Israel was in Egypt land
Let my people go.
Oppressed so hard they could not stand,
Let my people go.

> *Go Down Moses*
> *Way down in Egypt land.*
> *Tell ole-Pharaoh,*
> *To let my people go.*

When spoke the Lord, bold Moses said,
Let my people go.

If not, I'll smite your first born dead,
Let my people go.

> *Go Down Moses*
> *Way down in Egypt land.*
> *Tell ole-Pharaoh,*
> *To let my people go.*

(Sudden blasts of light. A jazz tune fueled by trumpets in the background. Sudden blackout.)

PRESENT PASSAGE: Beyond Borders

THE UNSEEN: *(As the storytellers amidst the humming drums.) Time is now. We are at the end of a narrow, hilly, winding road, just like a tunnel. But the length of this long road appears shortened with the assertive rhythms of African drums which fuel the soul of the black man on the road. The black man, formerly known as The Father/Griot/X, is now transformed to TRAVELER-X. He continues his journey, trailing this path of life with an unusual sense of urgency. You can tell this by obvious signs; the steady speed of his legs (a.k.a., "Lexus") as they slap and stamp their imprints on the beaten soul of the earth. The earth, in turn, registers her complaint. Or perhaps, affirms the message of the journeying one with the ooze of dust, smiling its accompaniment to a life-time crossing in the frontier of dreams. Sweat pours down from TRAVELER-X's brow as he struggles along this pathway, armed and encumbered with his lifetime belongings: an African drum, a trumpet, a few pieces of clothing revealing many eyes from the wear and tear of the years. They resemble the things smiling in the name of shoes around his feet. Twilight follows TRAVELER-X on this narrow path as birds chorus with trees, whistling, welcoming the stranger, or swaying and saying bye-bye to the black man on this journey of ascension. Suddenly, time changes. Flood lights. Flashing and blinking in front of the man amidst tumultuous shouts. Sirens from an ambulance. Rap music rippling in the air. And a church choir competing with the African drums now, being subdued by the multiple voices dislocating THE TRAVELER who now staggers, stupefied and groping amidst the darkness and the light: flashing, gazing, blinking, or closing their eyes until TRAVELER-X is completely mesmerized. In quick succession, a crashing sound, followed by a huge sign in blinding light spread in front of the man and accompanied by an oracular voice reads:)*

JAH ORISHA: At last, you have come to the end of the tunnel. Welcome! Welcome! Welcome to the crossroads! Welcome! Seven times, Welcome! At last you have come to the end of the tunnel. *(Silence, except for the heavy breathing. THE TRAVELER now overcome with fear is lying prostrate and groping to gather his belongings.)*

JAH ORISHA: *(Roaring like thunder.)* Who are you?

THE TRAVELER: *(Trembling.)* Ehm...em...em..."X".

JAH ORISHA: Your name is, "X"?

THE TRAVELER: Ye...yea..."X"...

JAH ORISHA: *(Calmer.)* Your name is "X"? "X" what?

THE TRAVELER: *(Thinking, trying to recall.)* Don't know. Don't remember... Hmn... Still trying... trying... trying... to find...

JAH ORISHA: *(Cynically.)* Trying to find what? Your Name?

THE TRAVELER: *(Stammering.)* Me... yea... I've... Been trying... To find it... To hold... Mighty One. I found it once... Twice... No! Then a third... and... and...

JAH ORISHA: *(Impatiently.)* Then what happened? *(THE TRAVELER is silent.)* Tell me. What happened?

THE TRAVELER: I... I... I lost it.

JAH ORISHA: You did what?

THE TRAVELER: I lost it!

JAH ORISHA: How? Your name lost, then found? Found, then lost again? *(Silence.)* Tell me, how? Who took it? Who found it? What was it the first time?

THE TRAVELER: *(Pensive, sighs.)* I don't remember. I've been dreaming. Dreaming too long... I don't remember.

JAH ORISHA: And the second time around? Recent?

THE TRAVELER: That too, Mighty One. The closer I am to the dream, the more I forget.

JAH ORISHA: Do you by any chance remember one Marcus Garvey?

THE TRAVELER: *(Confused, searching.)* Oh, Mighty One! That's me! That was my name in my other life. Praise, Mighty One! Thank you for the gift of Remembrance.

JAH ORISHA: And will you by any chance know Mandela?

Zik of Africa? Caesar Chavez? Rosa Parks and the likes of them sent to deliver my people in their hour of need?

THE TRAVELER: Me, too, Mighty One. I am everyone... all of them... my God. I am. I have been many people in my struggles through time and space. Crashing. Breaking down boundaries to take my people out of Babylon. Lord, Babylon is everywhere in the world today. Lord, why are there so many Babylons? Lord, I need an answer.

JAH ORISHA: It is the way of the world. Son, I didn't create Babylon. Ask yourself. Could I? Will I lay the hand of destruction on my own creation? Don't the Aniocha-Igbos say that a hen does not take the step that will kill its own chick? Answer me! *(THE TRAVELER is silent, dreamy.)*

JAH ORISHA: Son, you cannot find the word? You lost it? You lost the word? My word? I gave it to you! I gave you the word! Now answer me.

THE TRAVELER: *(Subdued.)* Hmmmmmm... Jah, I know. Now I know.

JAH ORISHA: So how did you get to become "X"?

THE TRAVELER: I lost my path, Mighty One. It's so hard, so hard to lead my people when they want to see with other people's eyes. It's so hard to lead when you're labeled the "outsider." When the hurdles are too many. And you dream to be home surrounded by the family with love. It's so hard when you get locked out in the cold without your family. Without love.

JAH ORISHA: It's hard, so you settle for "X." Is that your solution? *(Cynical laughter.)* So now, what do you want?

THE TRAVELER: My name. My place. Change my fate.

JAH ORISHA: *(Disgusted.)* I see. *(JAH ORISHA extends a hand to close the gateway.)*

THE TRAVELER: *(Frantically.)* God please, don't go! Don't leave me! I need you now! Change my fate. *(Showing, baring his palm to God.)* See? I have the marks. Too brown...I mean dark. Jah, don't you see they're fated? Nobody wants me except to serve them with these hands. God, I'm tired. Tired of serving others. Jah, I too want to be served. Jah, give me a new hand. I need a new, new hand. A brighter hand. What I have now doesn't reach far enough. They are too short. Stalky. *(Pause.)* God, will you give me a *lasik? Lypo-suction?* God, I need new lips. My lips? "Too thick," they say. Make them thinner, Lord. And my eyes blue. Yes, Lord! Give me blue eyes. Change my eyes from brown to blue. Maybe it will help. To change my image. God, I need it. But I ain't got no money. And no power Lord. And you know it. Jah, give me a new fate. Give me a new face!

JAH ORISHA: *(Mock, laughter.)* Child, "no money, no honey!" You know that child. That is your world... what they have turned your world into. It's not my making. Undo the world. If it must change, you must have a hand in it. You must become that instrument to shape its face. It's browning... everyday. Can't you see? Your world is changing color. Whether it's maturing, I cannot tell you now. But it's browning. And that's important. It's to your advantage. Son, be in your world, not out of it. Go and fetch it for *yourself...* Yourself! *(Gate is slammed against THE TRAVELER.)*

THE TRAVELER: Oh, please, please Mighty One! *(Prostrate.)* Don't please! Don't forsake me, please!

JAH ORISHA: *(Unlocking the gate, peeping out.)* So what do you want?

THE TRAVELER: I want my name. My name. Name me again Mighty One. I want my name back. As you can see, I'm here now. Let me in, Mighty One. Let me in. I need a place. I want my place. A place beside you... in heaven, Mighty One. You know... I've been traveling... been on the road for too long. Without a home. Without a place. Lord I want my place, beside you, in Heaven.

JAH ORISHA: I see. *(Pause.)* And you are sure you really know what you need, what you want now?

13

THE TRAVELER: Yes, Mighty One.

JAH ORISHA: First, you want a name?

THE TRAVELER: Yes, Mighty One.

JAH ORISHA: Then what?

THE TRAVELER: A place. At the center of the circle, Mighty One.

JAH ORISHA: That you had, but lost as you said. You have been Caesar Chavez, Rosa Parks, Garvey, Mandela, too! And now "X"? Deaf One. How come you lost your way? How come you lost your voice? What did you do with the legacy that I gave to you? What are you leaving behind for the seeds of tomorrow? My newcomer, tell me. What have you become? What happened to the name you inherited? Until you answer that, you will remain outside, the outsider. The road is thirsty. The stakes are high and heated. And the passage? Guarded. Stormy. Risky. And treacherous. To enter, to find your name, your place again, you must be ready to make your way through. Make your way. No one else will make it for you. Not even me. I cannot...cannot now promise to give back what is taken. For what is taken is taken with no promise of return. To return, you must be sure to find your way. For in your days, those who take do not give back what they take. The choice is yours; to lose forever, or take back what is yours. Take it. Take it from whoever took it from you. You cannot pick your name from the side of the road. You cannot pluck your name from the crossroads. You cannot pluck your name from the armpit of history. You are worth much more. Much more than history. You are *the history. Your name is history.* You must, you must find it. Wear it. And write it in the heart of the world. For now, that is my verdict. Good-bye, Traveler-X." (*JAH ORISHA vanishes. The gates shut behind. Sudden blackout followed with blinding light. TRAVELER-X screams and trembles. He is so frightened, his legs fail him and he falls prostrate on the ground. His belt loosens, letting his trousers wander while he is attempting in his panic*

14

to gather the things around his waistline. The black man is still on his belly but is struggling to look up to see beyond the blinding light, when he is again shattered by the roaring voice of JAH ORISHA and a beaming light.)

JAH ORISHA: Go! Find your name! What is your name Traveler-X? Stand! *(Echo of "Name-Name-Name" disperses. TRAVELER-X is trembling, teeth clattering.)* X, stand up! Up and dust your face! *(TRAVELER-X staggers, tries to stand up, but his teeth are clattering and his unsteady feet dance feverishly to some unseen drums throbbing within as he obeys the voice.)* X, stand! Welcome to the crossroads! Open your eyes. And your ears! Stand straight for I am with you. *(TRAVELER-X now more reassured, but with a questioning look, tries to steady himself. He still remembers to gather his belongings as he rises from the ground.)* Listen. Now listen, my man. You have come a long way not to know to listen. Now you are at the end of the tunnel. There are three exits in the tunnel. But first, let us get our bearings right. Where are you standing now? *(TRAVELER-X shakily, almost in the manner of a robot, looks around him. He sees various arrows and crossing of paths as in a market-square. He moves from the periphery to the center, does some kind of circling motion as if measuring his bearing with his eyes and responds in a near choking voice.)*

TRAVELER-X: Em... em... er... cross... roads... cross... crossing... crossings... crosses... roads... and, and crosses... *(UNSEEN VOICES in the background chanting: crosses-crosses-crosses! Crosses-Crosses-Crosses! While THE TRAVELER echoes, "Yes Crosses!" He is interrupted with a sudden harsh question from the mighty voice of JAH ORISHA.)*

JAH ORISHA: What crosses? Be sure of yourself!

TRAVELER-X: *(Nervous, hurried but soon re-assured.)* Cross-roads *(Coughs.)* Cross... Crossroads. I'm at the center of... of... *(Again stammers when the voice overtakes him.)*

JAH ORISHA: Now, well said. You have passed the first test.

At least you can tell where you are now. That is the beginning of your beginning.

TRAVELER-X: *(Alarmed.)* What?

JAH ORISHA: No questions yet. Now tighten your belt. And steady yourself. For again to remind you, you are at the beginning of the beginning.

TRAVELER-X: *(Tearfully.)* Again? The beginning? Always at the beginning?

JAH ORISHA: Yes!

TRAVELER-X: But... But... I've been going, going, going, and going all my life... And... and, still, I'm... at the beginning? Always at the beginning?

JAH ORISHA: I mean now! *(Brief silence as the TRAVELER gazes at the path he has been trekking as if trying to count his footprints on the path.)*

TRAVELER-X: *(Despondent.)* But how can I be at the beginning when I've covered all this distance? Can't anyone see these footprints? The dents of my struggle on the land? Can't anyone see that I too have made my mark?

JAH ORISHA: Granted! Your marks are at the beginning. Structured but not printed on the sands of time. Your marks left unprotected to the spirits of the market place. For you had too large a heart. Giving all. Taking none. Until you all were taken. Traveler-X! *(Emphatically.)* The spirits of the market place are hard bargainers. Hard, hard profiteers. Trafficking. Trafficking on human soul. Trafficking on human flesh. Trafficking on the dead, the born and the unborn. Black man, take note. Where you dwell is a market place. And you must trade like others to profit, not to lose. You must have a hard stomach to profit.

TRAVELER-X: How?

JAH ORISHA: Like the fowl, my dear one, you too must learn to swallow gravel to grind your food.

TRAVELER-X: I'm lost. I don't... don't understand anything

16

anymore…

JAH ORISHA: *(Interrupting.)* Hold it! Just hold it! And remember my words, for I am here for you. You must have a hard stomach, especially in these seasons of waste, wars, and wants to succeed. Construct your prints on stone, not on sand for others to copy or steal. Now, look where you're coming from. *(TRAVELER-X stares backwards.)* Can you see your footprints on the path as clearly as you left them?

TRAVELER-X: Hmmm…No!

JAH ORISHA: So soon? What happened?

TRAVELER-X: *(Struggling to find words.)* I… I… can't… Tell. *(Pause.)* Maybe stolen.

JAH ORISHA: Stolen? Again? Your marks stolen again? How long must the fowl feed into the goat's stomach?

TRAVELER-X: Not forever.

JAH ORISHA: Now, you have arrived. I must tell you that you may be better prepared for tomorrow. There's been a strong wind blowing beneath your feet to wipe off your prints from the face of time. That is why your footprints fade so soon. *(Brief silence.)*

TRAVELER-X: Hmm… I see. I see…

JAH ORISHA: Because you are tilling and toiling, forever tracing paths that are soon taken, and leaving you with none. Historical tunnels and treasures crushed and melted with your blood, your brow drips with sweat, wetting valleys of your cheeks along the zebra-crossing on your face.

TRAVELER-X: *(He feels his face with his fingers, daydreaming.)* Hmmm…

JAH ORISHA: Now you know, we can proceed! Traveler-X!

TRAVELER-X: *(Awakened.)* Here I am! *(THE TRAVELER is elated. Mixed blend of rock n' roll music, soul, jazz, traditional tunes, drums, and flutes rise, as if in rainbow colors spread along the path that TRAVELER-X has been trailing.)*

JAH ORISHA: Son, read the sign! *(TRAVELER-X reads.)*

JAH ORISHA: Where you're coming from, through the tunnel, is your world! It's a familiar ground. Needs no elaborate introduction. Now read the sign! *(Flashing everywhere, TRAVELER-X struggling to read.)*

TRAVELER-X: *(Clearing his voice, steadying himself.)* Em... Em... Route XYZ. INTERSTATE. PROMISES NO SAFETY. PROCEED AT YOUR OWN RISK! *(Alarmed.) What?*

JAH ORISHA: *(Laughing.)* The choice is yours! Now, son. This way on your left is ZERO EXIT. The shortest and easiest. It is called HELL! *(TRAVELER-X follows the description with his eyes and ears as the voice reveals. On Zero Exit, there is a bold sign in red which says, "Welcome to Hell." Behind the sign and penetrating the entire atmosphere of flashing lights at Hellsgate, a disc jockey appears rather business-like, as if performing the role of the Master of Ceremonies (MC). The disc jockey is a woman of color, SOJOURNER NKRUMAH.)*

SOJOURNER NKRUMAH: "Soul Train!" It's where the action is. Rap away your anguish. It's where the action is. Hell! Welcome to Hell. Freeway! Free ticket! Free parking. Hell got soul Broda! No worry! No hurry! No passport! No visa! Just come! Express! It's the freeway! Your freedom is our priority! Brother! Welcome to freedom! Free ticket! Free passport! Free visa! Free-free-free. Hell is fine music. It's where the action is. *(She is immediately overtaken by heavy, deafening rock sounds with neon disco-tech lights and silhouettes of people dancing. But no concrete shapes form. TRAVELER-X is enraptured in this familiar tune until the music snaps. Darkness overtakes Zero Exit and the light now shifts to the right, revealing "Heavensgate" with a steady shade of green. Again, the mighty voice returns.)*

JAH ORISHA: Son, welcome to the crossroads! On your right is Exit 739-436-3689...

TRAVELER-X: Exit what?

JAH ORISHA: 7-3-9-4-36-3689-Heavensgate!

TRAVELER-X: *(Overwhelmed, confused and rummaging*

through his bag for something to scribble it down.) My God, not so fast!

JAH ORISHA: Son, time waits for no one. You are on the cutting edge of time. So, if you must transcend it, just listen and learn. Now hear me. On your right is Exit 7-3-9-4-36-3689.

TRAVELER-X: *(Scribbling, sweating.)* My God! Why is the road to Heaven so long? Lord, please come again... *(Frazzled, he stops. Wipes his brow.)*

JAH ORISHA: What impunity? Taking me for granted? You're charged with the sin of distraction!

TRAVELER-X: Oh, Jeee! Another sin already? Where do I go from here?

JAH ORISHA: Again remember. Open your ears wide.

TRAVELER-X: I under... NO! NO! NO! I will understand.

JAH ORISHA: Now, hear me. On your right is Exit 7-3-9-4-36-3689...

TRAVELER-X: *(Scribbling and feverishly repeating after JAH ORISHA.)* Exit 7-3-9-4-36-36-89...

JAH ORISHA: It's Heavensgate!

TRAVELER-X: *(Eyes lighting up.)* Heavensgate? *(Pause.)* Heavensgate? *(Pause.)* Heavensgate! Exit 7-3-9-4... *(Singing, dancing in celebration.)* Heavensgate! At last! So long. So... so hard... *(TRAVELER-X looks ahead of him. Sighs deeply.)* Heavensgate at last! *(Picks up his load and lifts them onto his head with his right foot forward to move when the mighty voice again returns.)*

JAH ORISHA: Son! It's Heavensgate! You're at the doorstep of the mighty. Put down your burden. Bear not your load on your head, but on your shoulder. Lest you be crushed by the burden of life. Never carry the world's burden on your head, but on your shoulder, Black Man. Now you've seen it all. Now you've shifted base from edge to center. You can see it all and the choice is yours. You're completely on your own now, to make or break your world. It's my turn to take a vacation.

19

TRAVELER-X: *(Alarmed.)* God on vacation? How?

JAH ORISHA: *(Laughing.)* Of course! Gods, too, go on vacation. What did you expect? I'm just a God father. I am too tired... Too old...

TRAVELER-X: God? Could God too be old?

JAH ORISHA: *(Emphatically.)* Yes. Yes. Gods age... age and fall. Yes! Gods, too, die my son. Fathers demand paternity leave in your world today. Don't they? Son, your Gods are what you make them. Gods answer the names that you give them. It's the power you have, son. To name, even your Gods! Don't give up that power. Don't give up that glory to name and create your own world.

TRAVELER-X: What? Did I hear you right? Did you say power to create my world? But I have no such power!

JAH ORISHA: Now, shut up! *(TRAVELER-X, shaken, staggers and falls. JAH ORISHA speaks calmly again.)*

JAH ORISHA: I... I... I'm sorry, son. I didn't mean to hit you. I didn't mean to hurt you. I didn't mean to shut you up. But how can I, when I've been waiting? Waiting on the edge of time to hear you speak? How can I, when I see you like a brood of chickens in the rain with no mother hen to warm and house under her wings? I've been waiting to hear you for centuries. Even a hen shouts her protests and chases after the hawk who comes circling to steal her young. Even a hen sharpens her beak on the whet stone and sends alarm to the hendom. Alerting her entire community to protest assaults from the outsider who feeds on their soul. Even the hen has this power, how much more, you? *(Pause.)* Where has your voice gone? Son? Where has your poise gone? *(Silence.)*

TRAVELER-X: Oh, God! My God! More than you ever know, my soul is stabbed by your words. Much more than swords. My heart bleeds these seasons we failed to match words with deeds.

JAH ORISHA: Speak! The world awaits your words! Speak! Your brood awaits your words! With your words, stab the world's dead conscience to wake up and purge its heart of filth! Let's see what you do for yourself now that you know I'm on vacation. You have the power. Use it!

TRAVELER-X: *(Hysterical.)* I hear! I hear you Jah! You Gods! Ancestors! Ancestors I hear you! *(He goes into a frenzied dance. This is immediately followed with African drums and very hot rhythms which empower TRAVELER-X's feet so much that he dances to the hot tunes as he plays his trumpet. TRAVELER-X now brimming with confidence as he jumps and does acrobatic jigs. SOJOURNER NKRUMAH runs to the other side of the crossroads to join in the frenzied dance. But note that they do not meet. They are not aware of each other's presence. Each is alone, dancing for the self. Suddenly, a spotlight or searchlight, flashes on the right side. The light spots a man in white: white uniform, white mustache, white wings on his shoulders. He appears in military fashion. SOJOURNER NKRUMAH sees him, halts her dance and creeps back to her place beside the broken "Freedom Train." But TRAVELER-X is oblivious to all around him. Sirens follow. Then a voice superimposes itself against the mixed rhythms of the drums, now in chaos. STANLEY LIVINGSTONE appears. In the manner of the police, he starts writing tickets against TRAVELER-X.)*

STANLEY LIVINGSTONE: What the hell do you think you're doing? You mother f-N... *(The drums stop suddenly. TRAVELER-X freezes in mid-air, transfixed, not knowing who or what this new power is or how to deal with it.)*

STANLEY LIVINGSTONE: I say, where the hell do you think you are?

TRAVELER-X: *(Stammering.)* I... I... am...

STANLEY LIVINGSTONE: What are you? What are you doing here?

TRAVELER-X: *(Opens his mouth and closes it again.)* I... am...

STANLEY LIVINGSTONE: *(Impatiently.)* Now, get the hell out of here! Can't you see the signs? *(TRAVELER-X is suddenly jolted out of his stupor. He looks around him now, trying to read and study the numerous signs written boldly in every corner. Too many signals. A check-point with the inscription, "The Border: Watch Out/Aliens Crossing" is pushed forward to block the gateway. As he reads, STAN-LEY LIVINGSTONE presses a button and a pre-recorded voice from the instrument he wields blasts more orders. As the voice speaks, TRAVELER-X moves, confused as he tries to obey.)*

RECORDED VOICE: No standing! No turn on red! No entry! No trespassing! Single Lane! One way! Don't even think of parking here! *(TRAVELER-X has been reading all these breathlessly as each of them flashes until he loses his breath and gasps.)*

TRAVELER-X: Why? Why is the space so... so... so...taken?

STANLEY LIVINGSTONE: The space was taken long ago, black man! *(Pause.)* Where were you? Don't you know? What's wrong with you? You've been sleeping or what? Can't you see?

TRAVELER-X: *(Pause, staring at the signs.)* Hmmm... Heavensgate... *(More excitedly.)* Now, I can see... I can see now!

STANLEY LIVINGSTONE: *(Grinding his teeth.)* You better. Now, what can I do for you?

TRAVELER-X: *(Startled.)* But... but this is Heavensgate?

STANLEY LIVINGSTONE: *(Rudely.)* Yes!

TRAVELER-X: It's... its Heavengate..

STANLEY LIVINGSTONE: *(Irritated.)* Of course. I know it's Heavensgate. And that's all the more reason why I'm asking you the question, *(Picking his words.)* and Just In Case You failed to hear as you've failed everything else, "What-can-I-do-for-you?"

TRAVELER-X: *(More confident.)* Nothing. Nothing! Nothing at all!! This is Heavensgate. No one has any claim to it. I mean the space belongs to us all...

STANLEY LIVINGSTONE: Now shut up! So stubborn! *(Pause. Staring at him.)* You Sad... d... am...Sad... m ... Farrak... or something? Who says the space belongs to us all? Who are you? What are you, creature?

TRAVELER-X: Don't insult me any longer. I've taken enough already. One can only take so much. And we've taken so much. So much these five hundred seasons!

STANLEY LIVINGSTONE: Well, the sign is boldly written - Reserved! You need an entry permit. You need a parking permit. The space is reserved and you need a visa too!

TRAVELER-X: But this is Heaven! What do I need a visa for again? What credentials do I need again after centuries of struggle? Can't you see I'm worn and torn from the struggle? Can't you see I'm torn from toiling? *(TRAVELER-X's voice breaking down. Voices of the THE UNSEEN reappear, chanting in the background. In her own corner, SOJOURNER NKRUMAH mimes along.)*

THE UNSEEN: Toiling? Drilling? Trudging. So many Rivers... To cross-

TRAVELER-X: To... cross...

THE UNSEEN: To cross-

TRAVELER-X: So many valleys!

THE UNSEEN: To cross-To cross-To Cross-Crosses-Crosses-Crosses! Crosses! Crosses! Crosses! *(Echo of "crosses" swell. TRAVELER-X and THE UNSEEN do a duet.)*

TRAVELER-X: So many... so many. When will a man walk without cares? When will a man walk without looking over his shoulder for the unseen clubsman?

THE UNSEEN: Crosses-Crosses-Crosses!

TRAVELER-X: When will a man walk in God's own country without seeking parking permits?

THE UNSEEN: Yes, brother. Crosses! Crosses-Crosses-Crosses!

TRAVELER-X: Without paying for spaces stolen?

THE UNSEEN: Crosses Sistuh, Crosses! Crosses-Crosses-Crosses!

TRAVELER-X: Without proving identities?

THE UNSEEN: Crosses-Crosses-Crosses!

TRAVELER-X: Without licenses. Without insurances. Without labels. Without tags. Without-without-without?

THE UNSEEN: Crosses-Crosses-Crosses!

TRAVELER-X: Affirmative Action and labels of Black and White and Green and Red?

THE UNSEEN: Crosses-Crosses-Crosses!

TRAVELER-X: Why this color mania in God's own country? Why this color phobia in God's own country?

THE UNSEEN: Crosses-Crosses-Crosses! Crosses-Crosses-Crosses! *(TRAVELER-X's hysterical.)*

TRAVELER-X: *(Wailing.)* I paid my dues! Paying parking permits and entry permits! Hearing commercials and seeing images of us assaulted on T.V. Don't you think I've paid enough? To last my kind forever? Don't you think I've paid enough? We've paid enough?

THE UNSEEN: Don't you think? Don't you? Don't you think? *(THE UNSEEN chant until they fade out with SOJOURNER NKRUMAH.)*

STANLEY LIVINGSTONE: *(Arrogantly replies in a sing-song manner.)* Too bad if you've made a bad venture. Too bad if your investment hasn't paid off. Too bad you don't know the rules of the game...

TRAVELER-X: A Game? Which game are you talking about?

STANLEY LIVINGSTONE: Life!

TRAVELER-X: *(Repeating to himself, thinking.)* Life? A game too? So why is everything such a game? So many sports? Why's life such a sport? *(Pause.)* Am I a sport too for the champion to play me out and get a trophy on my account?

STANLEY LIVINGSTONE: *(Admonishing.)* Don't put it so crudely as you do everything else. Perhaps you're misled by my truth.

TRAVELER-X: Led by your mis-truth!

STANLEY LIVINGSTONE: No. I mean by my attempt at the

truth! Or rather, my directness. So, to help your failing senses, let's simply say that "Life is a School."

TRAVELER-X: Hmn... So "Living is Schooling?"

STANLEY LIVINGSTONE: *(Excitedly.)* That's it! Hmm! That's it boy! For once you've made an attempt to put something right and hit the truth on its head.

TRAVELER-X: Truth bleeds in your mouth, always...

STANLEY LIVINGSTONE: Now, you're going off the mark again. You're such a child. Just one word of encouragement, and you go off the mark, never weighing the ends. Limits must be measured.

TRAVELER-X: By you alone? So that you can keep hoarding everything and seize the key to the gateway?

STANLEY LIVINGSTONE: *(Pretending that he didn't hear the question.)* No! Back to the issues. The simple fact is, you don't know, and you will never know this market culture. Life's commercial. Capital. Commodity. You see? And this is a rehearsal, an opportunity for infomercial, if I may say. Doubt it? Ask the guber-presidential candidates. Ask them how they made it. Like all economic ventures, you either win or lose. Even when you play, like the game of cards, you got to play the right card or you lose.

TRAVELER-X: *(Screaming.)* But I've been losing!

STANLEY LIVINGSTONE: *(Grinning.)* Well, my boy. Some are born to lose... you know. Like you... And some, like me... born to win. You know, the chosen ones? It's a birthright. Too bad you chose the wrong color.

TRAVELER-X: But I didn't choose my card.

STANLEY LIVINGSTONE: Well, the fact is, you got the wrong color. You've got no green card. And you've got a black card. Boy black is too dense a color in the fog and the maze of streets. You can't see far, 'cos your card is too dense. It shields light for easy passage on the streets. For the license to sell, you need a card that's light, green and hopeful.

TRAVELER-X: *(Thinking.)* Like the dollar?

STANLEY LIVINGSTONE: Yeah-sort of! *(Brief pause.)* If you're not a dreamer. Which of the street lights in New York reflects the color black? You got Red, You got Yellow, You got Green. All these are lights, lights! Structured with us in mind.

TRAVELER-X: So I was never in the picture?

STANLEY LIVINGSTONE: Never in the picture!

TRAVELER-X: At all?

STANLEY LIVINGSTONE: Never in the dream!

TRAVELER-X: I see...

STANLEY LIVINGSTONE: Hopefully. Ehm, well... But from what I see, your stomach is too soft.

TRAVELER-X: What do you mean, my stomach is too soft? You take possession of my stomach too?

STANLEY LIVINGSTONE: Wait a minute! Don't go off on a tangent yet! What I mean is, your race is soft. Your stomach is soft, letting everything and everyone in. Lacking the gravel to grind the stuff. You know what I mean? LIFE-and all that? You can't run a culture on charity and hope to profit, my boy! And that's what YOUR PEOPLE have been doing for centuries: Open doors and new doors that lead to nowhere. New tunnels. Passages and passages *(He begins singing the familiar tune: "Upside Down.")* You see? Middle, upside down, inside out. Life's turning you. So you never reach the end of the road, and say, "Yes, I have arrived." You always going and never getting there. 'Cos you run everything on charity: Culture, Tradition, Religion, Language, Tongue, Politics, Economy, History. Even image-making. Myth-making. Marrying yourselves away. Your heroes, you give away. And give power to strangers and outsiders. No contest. No contest. So what do you expect? So what mortal sins have you not committed against your God? Against yourselves? I got to drum this fact into your blockhead, since it's only the language of the drum that you understand.

For once, let's indulge you by talking to you.

TRAVELER-X: *(Attempting to reply but he is in pain.)* Oh, God! My God! My stomach gripes. My heart's bleeding. Your punches are too hard. Too hard! Oh much too hard! But I'm seeing now the facts of history. *(THE UNSEEN voices arise, they chant the theme song, "History's Art, Not a Fact." As the voices mellow, TRAVELER-X rises into spiritual chant/possession.)*

TRAVELER-X: I hear! Hear! You Gods, You Gods, Ancestors! I hear you! I'm ready! Now watch me weave your story for posterity. That you – we – us - shall never again lie cold in this wind blowing to wipe us out! I hear you-I hear you! I promise. And to prove it, now watch me mount your faces on golden frames! *(TRAVELER-X rummages in his bag and brings out ancient masks from his homeland. Mounts masks on the blockade at the gates of Heaven and stands back to admire the face of the mask. Tilts his bag and brings out a small gourd containing palm wine. He pours libation on the ground as he chants incantations and takes a sip. THE UN-SEEN return with hot rhythms of the African drums. TRAVELER-X's feet now empowered: He dances, transformed into the figure of a priest or divine prophet. He is still dancing when the "SHERIFF" returns and yells at him. The drums are silenced. TRAVELER-X stands again bemused and frozen. STANLEY LIVINGSTONE takes over.)*

STANLEY LIVINGSTONE: Even in jail you disrupt the order! *(Silence.)* Do you realize you're disturbing the peace? *(Silence.)* There goes the man who sold his tongue for sausage and Swiss rolls.

TRAVELER-X: *(Incensed.)* But... but I paid my dues, I've paid my dues to last my kind forever. Don't you think I — we've paid enough?

STANLEY LIVINGSTONE: *(Arrogantly.)* Too bad. Too bad. I'll say it over and over again. Too bad you don't know the rule of the game. Too bad your lips are too thick to speak the sleek sounds of Francs, Sterling, Euro, and

27

the Dollar. Too bad you're so out of fashion matching white teeth with a black body. *(Smiling.)* To get ahead, you got to have sharp teeth. Teeth tinted in gold or sterling to get ahead. You got to be dogmatic with the green eyes of the dollar. Too bad you don't know you gotta have some good, good grand... life too is serious business. And dogmatic, you know- like the dollar? You either win or lose. Some are born like you, to lose. Some are born like me, to win. *(Laughing.)* HA! HA! HA! *(Flexing his muscle, he makes a dignified walkout.)*

TRAVELER-X: I don't lose from lack of trying! Indeed I've tried and tried! So many times tried and failed! For there are too many falls to survive! For there are too many winters after fall!

THE UNSEEN: *(Voices in the background.)* And spring's too far... And spring's too far...

TRAVELER-X: *(Startled.)* Did you hear that? I've been, I've been oh, so many seasons! Crossing rivers and deserts and forests! In monsoons, tropical and temperate zones. I've seen the color of failure. I know the color of shit. I know failure. Failure's an orphan. Failure knows me and here I am to say "no!" Here I am to say "no" to failure! Here!!

THE UNSEEN: *(Chanting.)* Here! Arise! Arise! Say "no" to failure. To failure-to failure! Reject! Reject! Arise! Arise! Say "no" to failure!

TRAVELER-X: No! Failure! Not me!

STANLEY LIVINGSTONE: *(Returning.)* HA! HA! HA! You kidding, boy? You wanna go to heaven without dying? You gotta learn to fall and rise like a child toddling and falling until his feet gain the power of height. So much so, that when he rises to walk he already associates rising with falling!

THE UNSEEN: *(Chanting in the background.)* You fall to rise! You fall to rise! You fall to rise! *(Thunder clap. TRAVELER-X jolted, staggers. Rumbling from the skies.)* Get up and go! Get up. Get up and go. You fall to rise. You fall to rise. Get up. Get up and go. *(TRAVELER-X startled and tired, stumbles and falls on his stomach. Tries to stand and steady himself but there is the mocking laughter of STANLEY LIVINGSTONE combined with thunder in the background. As STANLEY LIVINGSTONE is disappearing, he flips his fingers around his ears as if mimicking the movements of a bunny rabbit, puffing his cheeks.)*

STANLEY LIVINGSTONE: *(Mocking falsetto voice.)* "I've paid my dues. I've paid my dues. Isn't that enough?" *(Stages a majestic walk-out. He waves his hand and light snaps off. TRAVELER-X, now in total darkness, gropes and groans alone. Slowly stars begin to appear as the drums and THE UNSEEN voices rise slowly, chanting a familiar tune in the distance.)*

STANLEY LIVINGSTONE: *(Off stage.)* Better get your ass together. I hear voices. *(Stepping out to inspect.)* Newcomers, maybe. *(To TRAVELER-X.)* No loitering, understand? Just don't litter the path with your dead, drunk body. *(Roaring.)* Get the hell out of here!

THE UNSEEN: *(Chanting.)* Remember. Remember. Remember what he says. The new motto. The new order. Remember what he says. "Life's a game. Life's a business. You can't run life on charity and hope to profit." You can't run culture on charity and hope to profit. Even Heaven's run on profit. Even life's serious business. And Heaven's serious business. You must earn it. You must earn it. You must earn it. *(Drum sounds follow.)* You must work it - Duum! You must work it - Duum! You must name it - Duum! You must have it - Duum! You must pass it - Duum! *(Drum accolades, shekere, rattle beads, saxophones, horns, xylophones and flutes. Drum voices followed immediately by JEFFERSON LUGARD. He checks the scene as a policeman, smacking his lips as he drinks from a bottle, then exits.)*

STANLEY LIVINGSTONE: Too bad you're skin's too dark. Much too dark to blush in the sun. Too bad you've walked so far and gone not far, as you have done, always!

TRAVELER-X: I'm here to tell my story. I've come this far to tell... to tell my own story and write it too...

STANLEY LIVINGSTONE: I warn you, boy. Clear the hell out of here! This is the Garden State! There's the neighborhood watch. No loitering. You hear me?

TRAVELER-X: You talking to me?

STANLEY LIVINGSTONE: Sure.

TRAVELER-X: No boy here. I am a man... thirty-nine odd years...

STANLEY LIVINGSTONE: Your business, not mine. *(Pause.)* But I must warn you. This is the Garden State. Boy, to be honest with you. *(Pause.)* The mortgage is out of range for your kind. The space is reserved. Any more word from you and you get a ticket for trespassing. No! For breaking in, rather.

TRAVELER-X: Breaking into what? What makes you think you have the right to call the shots, always? *(STANLEY LIVINGSTONE raises his gun and aims at the black man who defends himself with his trumpet and hand knuckles. Then STANLEY LIVINGSTONE starts writing him a ticket. TRAVELER-X is now visibly agitated. When STANLEY LIVINGSTONE is done writing the ticket, he stretches his hand to issue it, but TRAVELER-X just stares at him like a lion about to pounce on its prey.)*

STANLEY LIVINGSTONE: Take it and get the hell out of here! You Prince of Darkness. You backward race! Backward in time! Backward in space! Backward! Backward! *(They are poised to attack each other. STANLEY LIVINGSTONE with his gun and TRAVELER-X though unarmed, arrests him with the fire in his eyes.)*

TRAVELER-X: *(Furious.)* Get off my back, sucker! Racist!... Mother F... You see this skin? Better don't mistake it for some leather to be worn by you. For I tell you, I got fire beneath this skin. And fire burns. Fire burns! Any more assault and it will burn you. You will be struck dead. By the thunderous voices of the ancestors lying beneath the depths of my skin, don't! Don't poke the jaw of the lion lest it spits its fire! Don't! This skin shines. Shines with seasons of polished pain. It shines. Swells. With soot from years. The many years of broken promises. *(Brief silence. He advances towards STANLEY LIVINGSTONE who retreats.)* And pain of partings of families? Ugh... Don't! Don't! Don't you dare! Dare mistake my ebony for some lightweight white wood. You woodpecker! Dare! And the birds will swarm around you. Turn your pale skin to straw for their new nest. Dare. Dare. Lay your leprous hand on me again. Sucker! And my ancestors Amadioba, Sango and Ogwugwu will strike you with thunder for centuries of abuse!

STANLEY LIVINGSTONE: *(Furious.)* Now shut up, you monkey! Shut up! Who do you think you're talking to? Now get it. No Affirmative Action in Heaven. Get it. This is no California. No Los Angeles. City of Angels for the Kings and riots. Not Palestine, Baghdad or LA where saints riot. Ok! Now forget Affirmative Action. I got Proposition 209 on board. You poised to vote? We won before the vote. Ha! Ha! Ha! It's on paper. It's on the ballot. There's no room for you in this region! No projects. No ghettos reserved for you. *(Pause.)* You think you can come here to mess up Heaven as you did Harlem, Lagos, L.A., Dallas, London, Newark, Detroit, Johannesburg, eh? You think you can assault the Heavens with your odious presence? (Pause.) Why can't you just return and take the back seat where you belong?

TRAVELER-X: God created all men equal.

STANLEY LIVINGSTONE: *(Mock laughter.)* Oh, yes he did, indeed. Ha! He did, you simple-minded folk. No wonder they say you're a race of juveniles. Hasn't it ever occurred to you that God is a politician like everyone else? When will you learn that men are just political animals. God made man in His own image, so that "Good Book" says. Or is it that man made God in his own image? Whatever! Makes no difference. *(Pause.)* So my fella, can't you see, that is the name of the game? God can't be so far from his own creation? Why can't you learn the game of life? *(Emphatically.)* Politics! Politics!

31

Politics! Life's seasoned in politics, stewed in diploma-cy. Hear! God is no different, though higher than man. God too is a politician.

TRAVELER-X: *(Confused.)* But... but men lie. God loves. I spoke with God this morning. Jah made me promises. Gave me assurances to be with me, now and always. Jah told me that since I've come this far, the space is mine. God's condition? That I must speak my own voice. I must insist on being heard.

STANLEY LIVINGSTONE: Oh, poor thing! How can I tell you that Jah is a ruler. Like all rulers, Jah too is a politi-cian? Can't you read between the lines?

TRAVELER-X: But it's written in black and white.

STANLEY LIVINGSTONE: What is written in black and white? You colorphiliac! No pun intended. *(Laughs.)*

TRAVELER-X: You colorphobic then?

STANLEY LIVINGSTONE: *(Irritated.)* I say no pun intended. Isn't that enough? *(Calmly.)* I forget you're too dark toned. That gets in the way sometimes. You're just too thick. Too thick in the head and skin. And oh, too much tone and pigmentation in the eyes. You can't see clearly. What can it see beneath the pale surface? But I'm willing to help you in your drift. *(STANLEY LIVING-STONE digs into his pocket and brings out a bundle of keys.)* Now look at these. You who have eyes but can-not see. If the maker were so just, why did he give me the keys? *(TRAVELER-X exasperated.)*

TRAVELER-X: No one gave the keys to you! Jah went on va-cation with Peter! You stole them! You liar! You stole them! Space, Soul, Life... What the hell? You think you can blindfold us forever?

STANLEY LIVINGSTONE: *(Arrogantly.)* Just too bad for you. You're already a lost generation. It's a pity, you'll never understand the logic of equality. The air you breathe, smells of politics. The water you drink, tastes of poli-tics. The grounds you walk, tarred with politics. *(THE UNSEEN voices return in a slow, low chant in the back-*

ground – *"Politics, Politricks, Politics, Politrics.")* This you'll never ever understand. But I got the keys. The creator went on vacation and gave me the keys. Or how else do you think I keep the gates of Heaven?

TRAVELER-X: *(Silently reflecting.)* So, you claim the creator handed the keys over to you?

STANLEY LIVINGSTONE: Yes! Just before he traveled.

TRAVELER-X: *(Confused, lost.)* Jah did?

STANLEY LIVINGSTONE: I said so already.

TRAVELER-X: Oh... Oh... my ancestors...

STANLEY LIVINGSTONE: Your ancestors are not in heaven. Your tribe is not represented in heaven. Don't even think that Affirmative Action can qualify you for this too. Any more noise and the President will enforce his veto Power.

TRAVELER-X: But this is where democracy should be most effective in the universe! *(Resignedly.)* I'm tired.

STANLEY LIVINGSTONE: Of De-mo-crazy! Ha! Ha! Ha! Better get moving now. It's the hour of our housecleaning.

TRAVELER-X: What? Housecleaning? I thought this was Heaven?

STANLEY LIVINGSTONE: Yes? So what? Move or I'll move you! *(TRAVELER-X angry, resists the assault. STANLEY LIVINGSTONE blows his whistle. A clanging noise is heard. The doors of Heaven open. LADY JEFFERSON LUGARD, a blonde heavenly woman, brings out a pail containing some dirty, foaming water from her laundry and suddenly begins to spew it on TRAVELER-X, almost blinding him. TRAVELER-X struggles to find his way. The heavenly woman walks seductively, hanging her under-wear and lingerie at Heaven's gate, while TRAVELER-X struggles to clear his vision. The lady, done with her laundry, walks seductively back into Heaven. STANLEY LIVINGSTONE watches her lustfully and smiles. Satis-fied with their achievement so far, he blows his siren. Heaven's gate shuts immediately with STANLEY LIV-INGSTONE departing. TRAVELER-X alone, trying to dry himself, exclaims.)*

TRAVELER-X: Oh, Jah! Where are you? Where are you? My Jah! Why have you forsaken me?

Why am I again rejected? *(Chanting.)* Rejected? Always rejected! Rejected in Heaven! Rejected on Earth! Rejected in life! Rejected in Death! Rejected! Rejected! Rejected! Rejected! Always rejected! Why! Why! Why! Why am I always rejected? Ascending, only to fall?

THE UNSEEN: *(THE UNSEEN voices rise up, taking up the chorus while THE TRAVELER leads the chant.)* Rejected! Rejected! Always rejected!

TRAVELER-X: Why do I rise only to fall?

THE UNSEEN: Rejected! Always rejected!

TRAVELER-X: Why? Why? Why?

THE UNSEEN: Rejected! Always rejected!

TRAVELER-X: Jah! Why am I so different? Why? Why? Why?

THE UNSEEN: Rejected! Always rejected!

TRAVELER-X: Jah, Why? Why is my skin so dark? It gets in the way of sight. Why? Why? Why?

THE UNSEEN: Rejected! Always rejected!

TRAVELER-X: Jah, Why? Why is my nose so wide? Spread so wide across my face, and yet, all air passes me and blows me by.

THE UNSEEN: Why? Why? Why?

TRAVELER-X: And in the race of the races, Jah, Why? Why? Why is my nose so wide? All air passes me by and blows me by or escapes and gets trapped by the faces of other races?

THE UNSEEN: Why? Why? Why? Rejected! Always rejected!

TRAVELER-X: *(Breaking into song.)* Why Jah? Why? For seasons I've tried. I'm tired of trying and crying.

THE UNSEEN: Tired. Tired. Tired.

TRAVELER-X: Tired of trying and dying!

THE UNSEEN: Tired. Tired. Tired. Trying and trying and dying for seasons. *(TRAVELER-X's voice drowns the chorus of voices as he sings a passionate solo. In the back-*

34

ground, however, the UNSEEN voices hum and affirm the TRAVELER's condition.)

TRAVELER-X:

For seasons, I've been counting.
Shifting and counting cards
To play black as the hit number in the rainbow.
The more games I win,
The more I'm played out in the row.
The more games I win, the more I'm played out in the row,
My cord cut-
As string to spread other colors in the rainbow
I hang out-
Knowing all else but me,
Finding all else but me, missing,
Al... ways...

Always... al... ways,
I find all else but me,
Turned around and around and around,
Shifted out of game,
Shifted out of fame,
Always...al...ways,
And made to lie

In limbo...

As colors advance in the rainbow,
Images of me crawl,
— Backwards, words back, back words,
Reflected behind clouds,
Or are simply summed up
With one harsh stroke of fire
Followed with zebra-crossings on my face —
And leaving me,
A riot of colors to firm up wind

Broken...

Where now is sure spot Left-
In the rainbow for me,
To spread the color, black

And not hang it?

Where now is sure spot in the wind,
Left for me
To spread the color black, and not hang it?

Too much color in winds-
Too much valor in winds, broken-

I AM COLOR.

Too much... too much...
Dyed, in winds colored and
Broken,
Scattering the race among faces rioting-

I AM!
So much, too much
My cord, strong, spread or scattered,

Defying wind-

I AM!
(Stops, groping.)

Jah, where are you? Why?
Why have you rejected me
For the thousandth time?
Answer me- me... meeee... Goooooooooood!
Jah, where are you?

(Explosive laughter. Music change. Drum blasts here.)

HA! HA! HA!

JEFFERSON LUGARD: Illegal Aliens in heaven? No way! Out! Out!

TRAVELER-X: What? Why?

JEFFERSON LUGARD: God is gone on vacation with Peter. And I... we are in charge here. We got the key to heaven.

TRAVELER-X: To heaven, too?

JEFFERSON LUGARD: Sure.

TRAVELER-X: Really?

JEFFERSON LUGARD: No more questions. Out! Out!

TRAVELER-X: But I was here before everyone else.

JEFFERSON LUGARD: So what? You need at least two forms of I.D. to get in (*Pause.*) Your Driver's License?

TRAVELER-X: (*Alarmed.*) My Driver's License in Heaven, too? Jeee... Emmm... I have none. How can I get a Driver's License when I'm locked out? Driven away? And I got no car? And I got no money? And I got no job? All I got to show, is this Social Insecurity?

JEFFERSON LUGARD: No! You're wrong again! The word is-Social Security.

TRAVELER-X: I know no Social Security. All I know is this insecurity. All I've seen is this Social Insecurity. All I feel is this Social Insecurity. But now Justice must take its course!

JEFFERSON LUGARD: Ha! Justice? What animal is that? You dreamer! Now get it. No Vacancy in Heaven. Or, you also want to overcrowd heaven like you did Harlem-New York, Milwaukee, Minneapolis, Freetown, Dakar, Watts-LA, San Jose, London, Lagos, Kingston, Soweto, Chicago, and... Hey you listen! You got to show your proof of citizenship. Your Residency Permit?

TRAVELER-X: (*Alarmed.*) What?

JEFFERSON LUGARD: Your Alien Number, duhhh! Don't waste my bloody time, boy! Yes. Your Green Card... "A" Number. Now!

TRAVELER-X: (*Rummaging through his bag and still holding onto the barricade at Heavensgate.*) No! Ehm... (*Frantic search.*) Ehm... here... I got a card. I got a card. See... Here... (*Offering his arms spread out.*)

JEFFERSON LUGARD: (*Inspecting the card, nose turned up. Loud laughter.*) You draw bad card, man.

TRAVELER-X: (*Alarmed.*) What?

JEFFERSON LUGARD: Yes, man! Wrong Color!

TRAVELER-X: But I didn't choose my Color.

JEFFERSON LUGARD: Well, too bad. Too dark... Black... Man

37

you need a card that's High, Hopeful and Bright.

TRAVELER-X: Hnm... You mean, like the Euro-Dollar... Pound Sterling?

JEFFERSON LUGARD: *(Chuckling.)* Yeah! Something like that!

TRAVELER-X: *(Pensive.)* Hnm... I see. But this is my card and it's black. I got a black card.

JEFFERSON LUGARD: You need a green card to go to heaven. That's the law.

TRAVELER-X: *(Furious, sing-song manner.)* I got not green card. But I got a card. I got a card, but it's black. What does it matter that any card must have color? What should I care that my card is green or red or blue or brown or beige? What should I care that any card is black or white? What do I care that my Card is Colored?

(Background Ritual Chant by SOJOURNER NKRUMAH with THE UNSEEN voices: "I got a black card!")

JEFFERSON LUGARD: Man, your card's got to be green for you to pass. No pass on red! *(Emphatically.)* No pass on red! Caution on yellow. You need the green card to life!

TRAVELER-X: *(Defiant.)* I got no Green Card. And I must live. I got a Black Card. And I AM living. I got a Black Card. And I must live. *(Provoking a call-response chant: "I got a Black Card."(THE UNSEEN and SOJOURNER NKRUMAH are the respondents, singing the refrain, "I got a Black Card.")* My Black Card is blue sometimes, I got a black card! My black card is red sometimes, I got a black card! My black card is green sometimes, I got a black card! I got a black card! That will be green someday, Green always! What do I care now if the sign is "delayed green"? And there are flashes of red or yellow? What do I care if there are multiple stop signs? All I know is that I must go. And go, I must! And pass, I must! And cross, I must! Must pass-Must pass! *(Heightened agitation.)* I feel this right of passage! I feel this rite of passage! Since crossing the Middle Passage! And pass, I must!! And Cross, I must! Since I got these crosses. Crosses-Crosses-Crosses. *(Rousing audience into Choral Chant.)*

CHORAL CHANT: Crosses. Crosses-Crosses-Crosses! Crosses-Crosses-Crosses! Crosses-Crosses-Crosses! Crosses-Crosses-Crosses!

(Suddenly realizing that he is not alone now and that his supplication is reaffirmed by others, he stops and gropes to hold on to something concrete. But all vanishes into thin air. THE TRAVELER is exasperated now.)

TRAVELER-X: Jah, where are you? Why? Why have you rejected me for the thousandth time? Answer me—me... meee... Gooooooooood! Jah, where are you?

(At this point, THE UNSEEN voices can no longer be heard, but TRAVELER-X is still hysterical. Suddenly, in answer to his last question, "Jah, where are you?" the black woman swings by in her rags. She has a few feather plumes around her waist. Behind her dangles the tail of a horse. It's obvious that she is a mad woman, costumed in the most incredible manner that only the creative energy of madness can conjure. Her attire too reflects a riot of colors. She emerges from the left, Zero Exit/Hell.)

SOJOURNER NKRUMAH: *(Strutting.)* Here! *(TRAVELER almost paralyzed from this sudden apparition or new assault on his senses. He freezes. The woman takes a step or two in front of TRAVELER-X. She swings her talkative hips, turns her back as if doing a fashion parade and now stands face to face with TRAVELER-X, her hands akimbo.)* What is your problem, BROTHER? *(TRAVELER-X, startled, staggers and again attempts to stand steady. Repeating herself and more seductively.)* I say, what is your problem, Broda-man?

TRAVELER-X: *(Trembling.)* Ehm... m... m... mm...

SOJOURNER NKRUMAH: What do you mean, "ehm... m... m... mm...?" I asked a simple question. Can't you speak? What kind of man are you, who can't state your case? *(TRAVELER-X is silent. She looks at him pitifully and sighs.)* Hear me you unseen spirits. Have they not always called me the weaker sex? Now how come I can take it and take it and take it and hold and lock centuries of pain in my hands and hips, yet he can't? What did they do to you "broda?"

TRAVELER-X: Hmm...

SOJOURNER NKRUMAH: You let them take your voice? *(Silence.)* Answer me, loser! You let them take your voice and still call me weak? Dare. Dare call me weak again, when I'm just the only rags you've got. *(Pause. She goes over to him and strokes his chin.)* I asked a simple question, brother. And all you got to give me back is, "Hmm?" *(Sternly.)* As if my question is some raw egg, broken and left in the refrigerator to rot for centuries! I say, what is the problem, BROTHER? Or don't you have no words no more? Even to state your own case? Don't you have no guts no more, Broda? Even to break your own wind? *(Calmly.)* I say, tell me. Tell me. Let's see the problem to-ge-ther. Let's knead it together. *(She advances toward him as if hypnotizing him.)* Give it to me. We need each other, brother. Give it to me. To solve this problem together. *(Seductively and now in a Jamaican accent.)* Broda - Me is yur sistu... Brodaman. *(TRAVELER-X still stupefied, gazes into space. SOJOURNER NKRUMAH comes forward, waves her hand across his face to feel his sight. TRAVELER-X is suddenly awakened and tries to catch her hand. But she breaks away. Turns her back on him now and breaks into a soulful song which is accompanied by THE UNSEEN in the background. She does a duet with the TRAVELER, but once the tune is over, she steps aside, away from him. Now his interest is awakened, he moves closer to her, but she moves away each time.)*

TRAVELER-X: *(Stops pursuing.)* Now stranger, sister. Who are you?

SOJOURNER NKRUMAH: Sojourner Nkrumah!

TRAVELER-X: *(Pensive.)* Sojourner? Nkrumah?

SOJOURNER NKRUMAH: Yes, Sojourner Nkrumah!

TRAVELER-X: Sojourner? Father! Lord have mercy!

SOJOURNER NKRUMAH: Are your eyes so masculine they only see your fathers?

TRAVELER-X: *(Hesitating.)* Hmm... No!

SOJOURNER NKRUMAH: My name is Sojourner Nkrumah! Call me Sojourner Nkrumah!

TRAVELER-X: *(Still thinking.)* You sound so familiar... so familiar. Your voice sounds familiar. I'm trying... still trying to re... member... Sis... it's not so easy to re-member, you know.

SOJOURNER NKRUMAH: You mean you're short of memory. You race of short memory!

You know Sojourner? Don't you remember? I am So-journer, *the* Sojourner. Call me Sojourner Nkrumah!

TRAVELER-X: *(Recalling excitedly.)* Mama!

SOJOURNER NKRUMAH: *(Emphatically.)* No! Don't mama me now. I'm not your mama, but your sister. I *is* your sis-tuh! *(Silence. They stare at each other, he is humbled.)*

TRAVELER-X: Why not Mama?

SOJOURNER NKRUMAH: "Cos when you is mama, you give and give and get nothing in return.

But when you is sistuh, you get sometin from "Some-body" and from Broda too... *(She laughs.)* Now you re-member. We've been crossing. Crossing and crossing each other for years. Our paths, always crossing. Now that we meet, it's our time to patch the roads together.

TRAVELER-X: I see. *(Silence.)*

SOJOURNER NKRUMAH: Where are you coming from?

41

TRAVELER-X: Somewhere.

SOJOURNER NKRUMAH: I know it's somewhere, but where?

TRAVELER-X: Somewhere! Must we always name everywhere? Can't we just believe where I've been, that I've been somewhere?

SOJOURNER NKRUMAH: Oh, certainly! Certainly! Except I've come to understand that we must not forget the art of naming, always. We must not forget to name where we've been. To name where we are coming from. That we may know where we are going. The power is in the naming, you know? Or don't you think so?

TRAVELER-X: (*Reflecting.*) I see what you mean.

SOJOURNER NKRUMAH: So where are you coming from, Broda?

TRAVELER-X: Hell.

SOJOURNER NKRUMAH: (*Laughing.*) So, if you're from hell, then I'm from life? (*Pause.*) And what is your name?

TRAVELER-X: X.

SOJOURNER NKRUMAH: "X" what? (*She bursts into laughter.*)

TRAVELER-X: What's so funny?

SOJOURNER NKRUMAH: (*Stops laughing. Becomes serious.*) And I say, where have you been brother, that you don't know where I've been? Isn't it amazing, Broda? That we've been crossing each other so long without meeting each other? How then, without meeting each other, and without being together, Broda, do you hope to cross Heaven alone? Single and hope to walk into Heaven? Alone? Expect a welcome when you have an accent? When your skin is so black? (*Silence.*) And you bear the talking drum? And wear "dashiki, " "kente, " "toga, " and "agbada?" And walk alone? When you're told that your ancestors are not in Heaven? How do you expect your prayers to be heard in Heaven? How will your prayers be answered when you've got no ancestors in Heaven? When you don't come from a family of saints? BROTHER? Don't you think we've got to learn

42

the game better together? There's strength in numbers. Or what do you think is the logic of *their* New World Order? *(TRAVELER-X is so moved by her question that he moves closer to her. Thick silence in the atmosphere. TRAVELER-X soon tries to break the silence, but his voice is at first very shaky.)*

TRAVELER-X: Emm... sis... sister... Rupture... Sister, you've just ruptured the last nerve I had left. *(Pause.)*

SOJOURNER NKRUMAH: *(Smiling.)* Well, brother-rupture... Or, whatever. You mean... hemorrhage? Hemorrhage. Is that new to the race of color? *(TRAVELER-X is silent.)* Well, tell me! Is hemorrhage new to the race of color? Hasn't that been the reality? The history of color?

TRAVELER-X: *(Awakened.)* Ah! Sister Sojourner Nkrumah! You have the gift of words. He-mo-rrhage. He-mor-rhage! That's it! That's it! One word to sum up five hundred years of history; Hemorrhage! Hemorrhage is, Black History! Back passage. Middle Passage. End passage. In past life, I've been many things: Garvey, Griot, Mandela...

SOJOURNER NKRUMAH: So what do you want to be now?

TRAVELER-X: All! All that I've been. Can, and ever will become.

SOJOURNER NKRUMAH: Now, welcome brother, man, son! (She turns around, offers him her "tail" to hold. He ties the tail around his own waist and takes up his trumpet. They do a short, erotic dance together. And finally embrace.)

SOJOURNER NKRUMAH: Hemorrhage is the history of Color.

TRAVELER-X: *(Excitedly.)* Sistuh! Thanks! Thank you for the gift of words! *(Pause.)* Sojourner Nkrumah! You're the Earth Mother. Glad to be connected. And thanks for connecting.

SOJOURNER NKRUMAH: No need to thank me. I'm just as grateful as you are. Thank you for the gift of becoming.

TRAVELER-X: *(Reflecting.)* Becoming?

SOJOURNER NKRUMAH: Yes! Becoming. Listening. Without words, the ear dies a natural death. Thank you for being alive to words.

TRAVELER-X: Now, I am awake.

SOJOURNER NKRUMAH: And we are waking up, together... *(Pause.) She brings out her stuffed, restless baby doll and acts as if she's breastfeeding it. She cuddles it, sings a short lullaby to quiet it before laying it down to sleep and retiring to polish her broken down Freedom Train with the man accompanying her.)*

TRAVELER-X: Tell me, why are you like this?

SOJOURNER NKRUMAH: Like what?

TRAVELER-X: *(Awkwardly.)* Emm... I mean... Emm... *(Pause.)* I mean in... in... in rags... Pardon my...

SOJOURNER NKRUMAH: *(Exploding into laughter.)* Oh, that? No need to apologize. It's my choice.

TRAVELER-X: *(Surprised.)* Ehn? But... but...it's... it's... like madness.

SOJOURNER NKRUMAH: Well, what's wrong with madness? I am mad by choice.

TRAVELER-X: *(Shocked.)* You are what?

SOJOURNER NKRUMAH: I am mad by choice! *(Silence. TRAVELER-X fidgets.)*

TRAVELER-X: Hmm... Sister you're getting me confused.

SOJOURNER NKRUMAH: Are you confused child? That's not strange, either. Life's confusion. So?

TRAVELER-X: No. Maybe that's not what I mean. I'm struggling, struggling as you can see... I mean... I mean sister you're a mystery.

SOJOURNER NKRUMAH: That, too, is no problem. Life is a mystery. Like a crazy quilt, we must weave it together.

TRAVELER-X: But you have chosen madness. How can we put it together when you're crazy? We need sanity to make it together. *(SOJOURNER NKRUMAH again explodes into wild laughter and stops abruptly.)*

SOJOURNER NKRUMAH: That is where you go wrong, broda-man!

TRAVELER-X: How?

SOJOURNER NKRUMAH: How not? I told you already. I chose madness. Now what you need to know is not *How*, but *Why*. I mean the essence of madness. (*Pause.*)

TRAVELER-X: The essence of madness?

SOJOURNER NKRUMAH: Well, yes! Madness flavors life. I mean madness moves the world.

TRAVELER-X: Ehn? You create your own madness to dance with foxes.

SOJOURNER NKRUMAH: And you need madness to dance the dance of death. *(Pause.)* You need to be crazy to be sane here.

TRAVELER-X: What?

SOJOURNER NKRUMAH: It pays to be crazy here. *(Emphatically.)* Crazy! That's the word. The world is crazy, and you too need to be crazy. You need madness to create your world.

TRAVELER-X: *(Thinking.)* Hmm... like Mike... I mean Jackson... "I feel good." *(He does a James Brown jig.)*

SOJOURNER NKRUMAH: Whatever. But I just know that it pays to be mad. Ask the Igbos of the black world. They'll tell you about Agwu. Agwu is both the spirit of Creativity and the spirit of Madness.

TRAVELER-X: How come?

SOJOURNER NKRUMAH: Madness is the other. Madness is the other side of Creativity.

TRAVELER-X: *(Searching for an answer.)* I... I see... *(Suddenly giving a victory salute.)* I see now, sistuh! *(Pause.)* Your words open my sight. I've done many things in my life I cannot understand.

SOJOURNER NKRUMAH: Haven't I? Haven't we all?

TRAVELER-X: Well, mine is out of context. That's why I'm here now, dead!

SOJOURNER NKRUMAH: *(Laughing.)* Who says you're dead? Are you not Garvey? Are you not Luther King? Are you not Mandela? You're African. Africans never die. Ask the ancestors, the living dead. Africans never die. They just pass and continue to pass on forever. Life is an eternal rite of passage.

TRAVELER-X: Hmm... And is that why we must continue to journey without reaching our end?

SOJOURNER NKRUMAH: *(Angrily.)* What other end do you seek? Haven't you reached enough ends? Aren't you tired of ends? What other end are you seeking?

TRAVELER-X: What end am I not seeking? I died! Yes, I died! Isn't it obvious that I died? You died? And that is why we're here? *(SOJOURNER NKRUMAH is laughing hysterically now.)*

TRAVELER-X: I'm sorry, sister. But you stab me with your laughter.

SOJOURNER NKRUMAH: *(Seriously.)* I heal you with laughter. Laughter heals.

TRAVELER-X: What?

SOJOURNER NKRUMAH: Yes! Laughter is the ingredient of black survival. Ask Bill Cosby. Jay Fox. Chris Rock. You need laughter to heal the wounds of history. *(Silence. TRAVELER-X is pensive.)*

TRAVELER-X: Yeah! Sister. I think you're right. Laughter is the needle to prick the dead conscience.

SOJOURNER NKRUMAH: *(Excitedly.)* Now you're talking, brother! You got it! You got the song of life! Sing it! *(TRAVELER-X blows his trumpet and begins to play a fine jazz tune briefly, then stops.)*

TRAVELER-X: *(Holding SOJOURNER NKRUMAH.)* You know, sistuh?

SOJOURNER NKRUMAH: What?

TRAVELER-X: It's good to be connected...

SOJOURNER NKRUMAH: *(Holding him.)* Reconnected. No! Interconnected.

TRAVELER-X: Yes, connected, reconnected, interconnected — All! You've opened my eyes to history. And I'm gonna tell you a story, my story! How I came to be here. Dead! *(TRAVELER-X sits, pulling SOJOURNER NK-RUMAH down to sit with him.)*

SOJOURNER NKRUMAH: No! Dead, no! Haven't I told you, you are not dead?

TRAVELER-X: But I've crossed the limits of life!

SOJOURNER NKRUMAH: You... we are going through the rites of passage.

TRAVELER-X: In Hell?

SOJOURNER NKRUMAH: At the crossroads. Too many roads to life. Too many roads to life. But the choice is yours. And mine.

TRAVELER-X: Well, let me tell you how I came to be here.

SOJOURNER NKRUMAH: *(Excitedly.)* Go on and tell! *(TRAVELER-X is silent.)*

TRAVELER-X: *(Clearing his throat.)* You know, I feel like an outsider. I've been an outsider. Or rather, those who call the shots made me so...

SOJOURNER NKRUMAH: Haven't they made us all?

TRAVELER-X: Yes. But sister, yours is different. You have a chance.

SOJOURNER NKRUMAH: To do what? Laugh or die? *(She laughs loudly.)*

TRAVELER-X: This is serious. Think of the black man in the new world. Always pushed outside. Rushed outside. Outside-inside. Except when he's an insider in jail. Sister, the black man in the new world has the throne of an insider in jail.

SOJOURNER NKRUMAH: *(Laughing.)* National tragedy! *(Pause)* How do we overcome?

TRAVELER-X: We are the tribe of outsiders. And that is the end goal of my struggle; to get to the center. To become an insider. And shape the cause of history. But history's course is not straight. I fell.

SOJOURNER NKRUMAH: How?

TRAVELER-X: Now hear my story! For years, I've been struggling. Toiling. Tilling day and night to become. But here I am as you can see, still on the road; a traveler in exile. Where do I begin? *(TRAVELER-X's voice is breaking down, but he persists. SOJOURNER NKRUMAH strokes his back to sooth his pain.)*

SOJOURNER NKRUMAH: You cannot give up now. The journey must continue.

TRAVELER-X: *(Sighs and continues.)* It's been a history of struggle. Struggling on the edge of time. Struggling. Struggling. Struggling. But never reaping harvests. For there was always another, reaping, reaping and reaping the harvests.

SOJOURNER NKRUMAH: Don't you sing me the victim-song. Don't you slap me with that victim thing. And tell me it's the way of their world; the modern. Haven't you cried enough? When will you get your act together and rise, Black Man?

TRAVELER-X: Aha! Well, I found out the very hard way. And decided I'll fight to be acknowledged, even if they denied me the profit. I made up a plan. *(Pause.)* You see. I used to go to this church. For twenty years, twenty whole years! I attended this church every Sunday. And for 20 years, I was treated as an outsider. I remained an outsider. The congregation was another tribe, or race – whatever. The minister belonged to them. I was alone, a minority in a minority. I knew it because there was no other like me that stayed on. Even when some like me stumbled there on the edge of time, they always went away, fast. Why? No one acknowledged their name or their presence. It was as if they never existed. But I persisted. Edged my way to the front pew in the church. For twenty years, every Sunday, after the service, the minister shook hands with members of the congregation. The congregation converged to chit-chat and salute at the end of the service. But they always bypassed me. They always bypassed me. For twenty years, no one appeared to see me. Not even the minister saw me on the front pew where he came to shake hands with everyone, but me. But I didn't give up, because I lived by faith. I walked in faith. "He'll notice me one day. He'll acknowledge me some day. He'll shake hands with me some day." But the minister never did. Neither did any other in his congregation. So, one day, I decided to find a way. "There must be a way, " I said to myself. So I went to a store and stole a big Mexican hat, you know? *(SOJOURNER NKRUMAH chuckles.)* A big Mexican hat, and I stole it! Next day, I wore this huge hat to the church and sat down in the front pew. All eyes turned on me. All eyes were now in my direction. But I pretended that I didn't see. I didn't see anybody. Even the minister was looking in my direction.

SOJOURNER NKRUMAH: Why?

TRAVELER-X: Men don't wear hats in the church. Through the entire service, especially during the sermon, he kept making reference to "these people" who assault the face of the Lord with their hats of evil. He said that many, many, many times. But each time, I smiled and nodded in accord with his sermon. Still the angry eyes stared at me. The minister persisted in his reference to the sons of evil. And I persisted in my silent defiance. At last, the service was over. Guess who the minister came to acknowledge first?

SOJOURNER NKRUMAH: *(Laughing.)* The hero!

TRAVELER-X: Me! I became an instant hero. The minister shook hands with me. Told me I wore a very fine hat. The congregation looked stupefied. They started crowding around me and whispering, "That's the man. That's the one who stole that hat! Jack's hat. You remember? That's him." Well, I heard them but listened to the minister. "Where are you from?" asked the minister. "I am from here, " I replied. "Are you?" "Of course, yes!" "But where have you been?" "Always here. Always been here." "It must be very recent." "NO!" I said. "I've been here, Always!! For twenty years, I've always been here, on this same pew in this same church. But no one appeared to see me." "I'm glad you came, " the minister

49

said. "I'm glad you see me now, " I replied. Then suddenly, behind me, someone twisted my neck, "Thief!" they shouted and pulled the hat. I heard a gun shot. I heard my own voice scream. Blood had ruptured from my head. I saw the minister laughing. I saw a million faces laughing. But they were colorless. Whatever else I saw is history. And I am here. Now...

SOJOURNER NKRUMAH: On the crossroads. *(TRAVELER-X breaks down. SOJOURNER NKRUMAH empathizes, goes over to embrace him. She blows into his trumpet as a way of urging him to play. He sounds a slow, blues tune. They begin singing when suddenly STANLEY LIVINGSTONE and JEFFERSON LUGARD storm the scene.)*

JEFFERSON LUGARD: *(Crossing them.)* Hey you, look here. Scandalizing the Saints? This is heaven you know. No monkey business here. Got it? This is heaven. Can't have you litter up the place with babies. Pregnant babies for that matter as you do always. You think this is Africa? India? Bangladesh? Baghdad? China or something? You terrorists. *(TRAVELER-X and SOJOURNER NKRUMAH ignore him and stay locked in each other's arms. JEFFERSON LUGARD approaches threateningly to give them a few jabs. Still, they hold on.)*

SOJOURNER NKRUMAH: *(Kissing TRAVELER-X.)* Won't you leave us alone?

JEFFERSON LUGARD: Leave you, alone? What nonsense! *(He advances threateningly towards TRAVELER-X.)* I say, leave that woman alone! And that's an order!

TRAVELER-X: *(Defiantly.)* Ole Massa. I can't. She's all I got. This woman is all I got. De sistuh is all I got.

JEFFERSON LUGARD: *(Pulling out his gun.)* Are you talking to me?

SOJOURNER NKRUMAH: *(Strutting away.)* Put down your weapon, white man. Or go find your enemy. We are not the enemy. Your enemy is nothing but yourself. Your fear. That is your enemy. Not us. Look at us. We are not armed. *(Baring her arms.)* See? We ain't got nothing. Nothing but us. Ourselves. That's all we got.

TRAVELER-X: Since you take all to yourself.

JEFFERSON LUGARD: You are jealous. That's all.

STANLEY LIVINGSTONE: *(Positions himself beside JEFFERSON LUGARD.)* Envy. Racial envy. That's all. All you need to do is become like us. Work hard.

SOJOURNER NKRUMAH: *(Disgustingly.)* Become like you? That Is Death! *(Walking away.)*

TRAVELER-X: *(Simultaneously.)* Rot! Decay! Yuck! Must everyone be like you? Where is the difference? Where is the polarity? Same. Same. Same. Sameness all the time. Look into the faces of your country. Are they all the same? So why this creed of sameness? Why are you so scared of difference? Anyone you approve of must be like you? Give me a break! Your bigotry stinks! *(He spits in disgust. Suddenly, STANLEY LIVINGSTONE fires in front, JEFFERSON LUGARD fires from behind. TRAVELER-X finds himself hemmed in.)*

STANLEY LIVINGSTONE: Lock him up.

SOJOURNER NKRUMAH: *(From a near distance.)* Lock him up for what? What is the charge?

JEFFERSON LUGARD: You crazy woman? Must I have a charge? Must I have a reason to lock him up?

SOJOURNER NKRUMAH: Well, you should. Isn't this a free country as you say? The greatest nation of all times? The land of freedom and liberty? *(JEFFERSON LUGARD looks at STANLEY LIVINGSTONE. They both laugh. STANLEY LIVINGSTONE whistles, checks to ensure that the security lock on the border is still intact, while JEFFERSON LUGARD arrests TRAVELER-X.)*

JEFFERSON LUGARD: Precisely! Because I got freedom. I have liberty. Both Freedom and Liberty belong to me. And I got justice too. I can do what "I" like. What "I" want. Yes, I got freedom, woman! So get off my back! Can't stand your... you stink. Just get the hell outa here! Back into your place! *(As he speaks, he closes in on her and begins to fondle her. SOJOURNER NKRUMAH winces and cries out loud. TRAVELER-X can see it all from his*

51

space or jail across the border. He struggles to extricate himself and run out to rescue her, but his effort is in vain. In frustration, he groans.)

SOJOURNER NKRUMAH: Auch! Ugh! Get your bloody hand off my womanhood, you mother-f-s-o-b! Sucker!

JEFFERSON LUGARD: Hey babe, relax, and enjoy my freedom. *(STANLEY LIVINGSTONE still whistling as he approaches. JEFFERSON LUGARD embarrassed, turns away immediately. He binds her hands in chains. She resists and screams as he casts her beyond the border.)*

SOJOURNER NKRUMAH: *(Screaming.)* No! Let me go! Set me free! Not any more! No more! You can't put me in shackles any more. My God! My Ancestors! Cooooome!

TRAVELER-X: *(With a strained melody.)* Oh, yes, the Ancestors will set you free... set us free. Oh, Jah. They know it. We have seen enough. Had enough.

SOJOURNER NKRUMAH: *(Responding in song.)* Oh, yeah! My Ancestors. You brought them here in chains against their will. Your human cargo. *(STANLEY LIVINGSTONE and JEFFERSON LUGARD look in disbelief as they watch this duet. They make a sign to each other. The former doubles the chain on TRAVELER-X to secure him, while the latter reinforces SOJOURNER NKRUMAH's place at hellsgate.)*

TRAVELER-X: To do your labor...

SOJOURNER NKRUMAH: Pick your cotton...

TRAVELER-X: Farm your fields...

SOJOURNER NKRUMAH: Stolen from Indians...

TRAVELER-X: Indians slaughtered. Massacred for compost and manure to grow your capitalism.

SOJOURNER NKRUMAH: Indians crying out from mass graves in the Black Hills of Dakota... Wounded Knee. *(Pause.)* You remember Wounded Knee?

TRAVELER-X: Mexican fingers chopped off and sold inside the grape bags in California. You remember Chavez?

SOJOURNER NKRUMAH: Oh Yes! Oh Yes, Chavez!!

TRAVELER-X: And Japanese brains blown up and used for broth and stock in your Internment Camps...

TRAVELER-X: Hiroshima...

SOJOURNER NKRUMAH: Nagasaki...

TRAVELER-X: And my Ancestors?

SOJOURNER NKRUMAH: Oh, my Ancestors-Nubian, Mandingo, Malinke, Yoruba, Igbo, Ashante, Fante, Edo, Kikuyu, Gikuyu, Zulu, Ndebele... Oh, heroes of the Nile...

TRAVELER-X: Builders of pyramids...

SOJOURNER NKRUMAH: Iron and Steel...

TRAVELER-X: Nok and Nile culture...

SOJOURNER NKRUMAH: Great farmers...

TRAVELER-X: Great weavers...

SOJOURNER NKRUMAH: Great sculptors and painters who taught them all...

TRAVELER-X: Greek, Roman, Euro-American... *(STANLEY LIVINGSTONE and JEFFERSON LUGARD are visibly agitated.)*

SOJOURNER NKRUMAH: You mothers and fathers bound hand and feet...

TRAVELER-X: Their human cargo sent to the Carolinas...

SOJOURNER NKRUMAH: To the Americas...

TRAVELER-X: East, west, north, and south...

SOJOURNER NKRUMAH: Jamestown, Kingston, Haiti, Barbados, Brazil...

TRAVELER-X: Bodies mangled...

SOJOURNER NKRUMAH: Blood boiled in the Middle Passage...

TRAVELER-X: To propel the wheel and the machine of their progress...

SOJOURNER NKRUMAH: Oh, Yes! They rushed; like the gold rush in Indian land, they rushed. My people in chains... *(Growing tension, STANLEY LIVINGSTONE and JEFFERSON LUGARD move closer to each other and whisper.)*

TRAVELER-X: Dead, living, or dying in chains...

SOJOURNER NKRUMAH: Oh, what we have been through?

TRAVELER-X: Rivers... Rivers... Rivers! My Ancestors have known rivers...

SOJOURNER NKRUMAH: And I know Langston...

53

TRAVELER-X: "The Negro Speaks of Rivers." Langston...
*(Together, they turn the poem into song. As they chant,
their adversaries cannot stand it any longer.)*

STANLEY LIVINGSTONE: *(Aside to JEFFERSON LUGARD.)*
This is incredible. Are you sure they don't know each
other? Is this not a set-up to overthrow us? You think
they're spies? Terrorists?

JEFFERSON LUGARD: Maybe. You never know with these
people. You can't trust them.

STANLEY LIVINGSTONE: Always scheming; one thing after
another. Always something beneath the smiles, beneath the "Yes ma"... "yes massa"... No. These people
are black and black inside. That skin shades everything.
We must be on guard.

JEFFERSON LUGARD: Yes, watch. *(Singing and marching.)*
"Onward christian soldiers. Marching as to war." *(After
they sing, TRAVELER-X counters with another tune- "We
shall overcome, We shall overcome someday, " while SO-
JOURNER NKRUMAH responds with "Deep in my heart,
I do believe, we shall over..." JEFFERSON LUGARD shouting SOJOURNER NKRUMAH down.)* Shut up woman!

SOJOURNER NKRUMAH: You can't shut me up! No! Not any
more! You can't silence me. You gagged my mothers.
You gagged my fathers. Branded their lips. Burned
them. No! You can't do that anymore. In the past, you
did and got away with it. With murder. Now, you are
not free. You got no freedom so long as you hold others
back or down. No! That's the law of nature. That's the
price you pay. You lost your freedom when you took
mine. Now you carry a myth that weighs you down.
Yes, your freedom is a myth. Always has been. Stop
deceiving yourself. You too lost your freedom. You do
not have it!

JEFFERSON LUGARD: Oh that? I got it. I got it in my hands.
*(He quickly probes into his pocket and brings out the
Statute of Liberty and mounts it on a pedestal by the
border. He steps back and begins to admire the statue as
he speaks to STANLEY LIVINGSTONE.)*

JEFFERSON LUGARD: A beautiful one, don't you think? The founding fathers were great!

STANLEY LIVINGSTONE: Of course! Of course!

JEFFERSON LUGARD: And you remember the origins?

STANLEY LIVINGSTONE: Oh yes, of course! Got her from the Indians, Ehm... ehm... what did they say she was?

JEFFERSON LUGARD: *(Ridiculing.)* Their mother, of course.

STANLEY LIVINGSTONE: Oh, Indians! Poor benighted souls! Doesn't it amaze you how simple-minded those people are? Just like the savages in Africa. Tell me, if these people are not dumb, how can they have so much wealth — gold, steel, and all the mineral resources around them and not exploit it? They just sit by and watch us take it. Hey, I must give it to our fathers. The founding fathers were great heroes. Great entrepreneurs. I'm glad to be a descendant...

SOJOURNER NKRUMAH: *(Shouting as she tries to jump the border.)* Of murderers! Son of cannibals! Genocide... *(While she struggles to be free, they stare at her in disbelief. STANLEY LIVINGSTONE goes to recheck the border.)*

JEFFERSON LUGARD: *(Sighing.)* It's no point bothering your kind. You're mad already. So it makes no sense trying to put order in your place. You're already established. *(Laughing.)* In Hell of course! And that's guaranteed. This generation, next, and forever.

SOJOURNER NKRUMAH: *(Hysterical.)* You lie. You are not my God. You didn't create me. You don't have any power over me.

JEFFERSON LUGARD: *(Laughing.)* You drunk or something?

SOJOURNER NKRUMAH: My God will save me. Jah will come at the appointed time to redeem me... redeem us. Didn't God save the children of Israel? Didn't God bring the children of Israel out of Babylon? King of Babylon, we shall overcome. We shall overcome. *(She breaks into a song with the strained voice of TRAVELLER-X in the background.)* We shall overcome, we shall overcome someday. Deep in my heart, I do believe...

JEFFERSON LUGARD: *(To STANLEY LIVINGSTONE.)* I say shoot him. Or shut him up!

SOJOURNER NKRUMAH: What has the brother done? He ain't done notin.' Give me a reason why.

JEFFERSON LUGARD: Must I give a reason to shoot...? Must I have a charge?

SOJOURNER NKRUMAH: Well, you should. I thought this was a free country. The greatest nation ever, the land of liberty, freedom.

JEFFERSON LUGARD: *(Sardonic laughter.)* Precisely! Because I'm free to do what I like. What I want. Yes, woman. I got freedom. I got freedom. And you ask me if or why I must exercise that freedom! What a dumb question! You dreaming or something? Well, I forgot... you're colored. Colored folks always dreaming. That's how Martin got famous. He's drinking tea in hell. *(Laughs, stops abruptly.)* Seriously, we got him. Took care of him. Damn it! What did he think this country was about? A joke? What guts! Running his stinking mouth like that? What do niggers need a dream for?

STANLEY LIVINGSTONE: Soul food? *(They laugh.)*

JEFFERSON LUGARD: Eat and sleep. That's all they do. Eat. That's all they're good for. Lazy bunch of good-for-nothings. Go to the projects and see them. Sleep, buy Chinese food, McDonald's, Wendy's hamburgers. Name it! Negroes eat. Fart! *(He changes his voice to a rural Southern accent.)* See them projects in Harlem, South South Chicago, Bronx, Newark, Detroit-East. I tell yah. We got a problem with them niggers in this country. A whole race on welfare. And move those immigrants. Immigrants are like ants streaming, crawling through the border. Our borders are just too porous. And I tell you. Buchanan was right. The parrot too... Beg-yea pardon... Perot... That's what I mean, Ross. He too. But the "buck" *(Smart guy!)* said it outright– lock them borders and throw the key into the ocean to keep them out. And the Newt, bless his soul! Newt had it made. A better game plan if you ask me. Built them more orphan-ages and put them all in there... all them colored folks. Then they'll shut up. Just glad and thankful that you gave them one loaf of bread a day. Then they'll know the worth and value of them tax-payers wasting them hard earned dollars doling them out to keep them fat. That's what they are. If you doubt me, go to the inner cities. *(He lights a cigar.)* Sleep. That's all they do. So we did Martin a favor and put him to sleep– forever! *(Giggling.)* Nothing wrong with that. What does he take our nation for? A joke? Look, we're a nation of laws! Hear that? Laws! If you don't mess with us, we won't mess with you. But he got drunk on a dream. Poor guy, Martin... Suffering. Straining too hard to dream and think at the same time? That's too much. We saved him. Put him to sleep. So he can rest. Rest in peace...

STANLEY LIVINGSTONE: Pieces! *(Raucous laughter from both of them as STANLEY LIVINGSTONE exits.)*

JEFFERSON LUGARD: *(Alone, mimicking.)* "I got a dream! I got a dream!" Yes, he got a dream. And guess what? America put him to sleep. He never woke up. Dream choked him. Got drunk on dream, rather. Drowned and got buried in it. With it. Poor Martin. I'm sure he's still dreaming in his grave. Dream killed him. Poor thing. *(Pokes ashes from his cigar.)* Fools! Fools, all of you. And do you know what? Like a herd of cattle, Malcolm joined Martin. In the case of that charlatan, he wasn't just drunk on his dream. Dream turned him violent. Now you don't suppose that any right thinking man would see a madman desperately rushing on him and chanting, "By Any Means Possible" and stand there waiting for him to gun him down? Do you? No! That's against the law of nature. *(Chuckling.)* You get him first! Teach him a lesson. *(Stressing.)* "By Any Means Possible!" Precisely! That's what we did. Self defense. So what's wrong with that? History... and the law sanc-tions it. And I tell you, now from the ashes of Malcolm, another charlatan is rising. Ehm... what does he call himself? Far... Farra Arafat.... Sadd, and Chavez, that miniature Pyong, like a ping-pong ball, and now that Iranian terrorist leader with his nuclear dreams? Heretic! Blaspheming against God's chosen people! What an insult? When they get him, they'll blow his blasted mouth off. Display his blasted body at the Smithsonian. Dress it up in Halloween colors. Paint his face black like the true devil he is.

LADY JEFFERSON LUGARD: *(Joining him.)* A season of atonement. How in the world the colored think they can be saved? Have they got soul? How in the hell they wanna be saved without us? Without going through us. How are they gonna do it? We got the key. These people are in hell and they don't even know it. Keep dreaming. Always dreaming of things beyond them – like O.J. thinking he is gonna be free after the sinful acquittal! What pervasion of justice! If you'd ask me, I'd say all those mother f-black, jaundiced jury should have been thrown into jail without probation for life for their sin against history – letting O.J. out? That's the most unforgivable travesty against history. Our founding fathers were just. They would have blown off the heads of them tribe of N- Beg you pardon, but that's what they are — motherf-N-nonsense. And now they persecute our "foreman." I'm fed up. But do you blame them? It's them liberals in congress. Traitors against the founding fathers. Against our constitution, the best demonocracy in the world. Those eggheads... liberals... *(Spits in disgust.)* They're the worst thing that's happened to this nation. Preaching equality, Civil rights and all that jazz. Betray us. Come to the house and don't know a thing about them colored that they support. Don't they know that if you give the devil an inch, he wants a mile? That's it! That's the trouble we face today.

JEFFERSON LUGARD: The sooner or later we know it, the better. And then the siege of aliens at the border. Everyday, crossing. Sneaking through the border. Sneaking. Sneaking. Everyday! Aliens crossing. That's why we invented this. *(He shows the sign "Alien crossing: Beware.")* Well, know it. We're under siege. Alien invasion. Again in self defense, we vote more money to keep them out. Reinforce the border. That's why we're here. The Indians are already put away – in the reservations. No threat. The Russians, handicapped. No threat. Iraq. North Korea. And that China... Asia is our target. And Iran? We'll get them too! *(They laugh.)* You wonder why we vote more money for security than for education, Medicare and the environment? Nonsense. Security first! Without it, there's nothing. This is the freest nation in the world. Security is our business. That is why we must keep our nukes... assault weapons. Nobody dares to mess with us, or we mess with them first. Self interest. National interest, first. Million Man March – Million Man March! What the hell is wrong with them? What is the world turning into? Far... Farrak..! Feed him to vultures. *(Mock laughter.)* Watch it Louis! Dream gonna get ya!

LADY JEFFERSON LUGARD: Gonna get ya! Watch it! We're watching you. You riding too far, too fast. Beware of accidents on the road. Accidents are not always accidents, you know. Could be programmed. Trust us. Okay? Lest you end like Your kind — Malcolm, Martin. *(Pause.)* So woman, I'm not surprised that your people are all still dreaming. You are, after all, a tribe of dreamers. *(She leaves.)*

JEFFERSON LUGARD: *(Taunting SOJOURNER NKRUMAH.)* Woman, are you inside or outside this country? Wake up woman! *(Strutting.)* Behold freedom dancing in your face. *(He struts and gyrates.)* See? *(He points to the Statute of Liberty in his hand.)* See? I got it. Duh!! Woman, I have been here long enough to know your limits. You don't, and, perhaps, never will. But we'll knock it into you. Stay outside. Know your limits. And the colored man? Ha Ha Ha! Dead! The best of them are the dead ones. The living ones died long, long ago. It doesn't matter whether they're black or brown. They're all the same... these minorities. Fussing and fussing. Thinking they can force their way into any hole, through anything. Stumps they all are. Stumps! Want to enter at all costs. (*Pointing at THE TRAVELER.*) And see that one? See where it has landed him? Jail. Jail. 90 percent of the men in jail. No probation. We're working on that too. The president, the bloodiest of them liberals, just too, too liberally incompetent. "Three Strikes and You're Out." What a mockery of justice. That's too much. We're suffering from too much liberty in this country. Abuse of freedom. Three strikes! Why not once! Once, and you're out. In jail. Throw the key into the Atlantic or the Pacific. Or better still, feed their dark bodies to whales. (*Returning to SOJOURNER NKRUMAH.*) Woman, I don't owe you a reason, but just in case you want to be educated, hear the truth. You see that wall separating us? That's the border.

SOJOURNER NKRUMAH: You've said so much without meaning. Talk is cheap. Answer my question. What did the brother do that you had to lock him up?

JEFFERSON LUGARD: Woman, I don't owe you a reason. (*STANLEY LIVINGSTONE returns, pushes THE TRAVELER towards JEFFERSON LUGARD who holds a bigger lock. TRAVELER-X resists, struggles and tries to choke him. They attack him. As STANLEY LIVINGSTONE fires in front, JEFFERSON LUGARD fires from behind. TRAVELER-X finds himself hemmed in again.*)

STANLEY LIVINGSTONE: Lock him up. And throw the key into the Atlantic Ocean.

SOJOURNER NKRUMAH: Lock him up for what? What crime? The brother ain't done notin'!

JEFFERSON LUGARD: Attempted break in.

STANLEY LIVINGSTONE: No. Attempted murder.

SOJOURNER NKRUMAH: But you are dead. How can he murder you?

JEFFERSON LUGARD: None of your business.

STANLEY LIVINGSTONE: Now out! (*He shoots into the air in her direction. She runs for cover.*) Tie him up!

60

TRAVELER-X: *(Screaming.)* Let me go! Let me go! This is unjust. It's unjust! *(THE UNSEEN, masked and acting as the heavenly bodies run out to find out what's happening.)* What do you think you're doing? Where is this?

STANLEY LIVINGSTONE: Heaven.

TRAVELER-X: *(Shouting.)* Lie!

STANLEY LIVINGSTONE: Your Heaven is a lie? *(TRAVELER-X tries to hold back STANLEY LIVINGSTONE's hand as he ties him up. He sprays some chemical to knock out or sedate SOJOURNER NKRUMAH. She soon begins to snore.)* Dare! *(THE TRAVELER aims at STANLEY LIVINGSTONE's throat.)* Dare! *(STANLEY LIVINGSTONE fires into the air. TRAVELER-X frightened, freezes.)*

LADY JEFFERSON LUGARD: *(Running in with her night clothes, almost half-naked.)* What the hell is going on?

JEFFERSON LUGARD: *(Calmly.)* Nothing, darling. No problem. *(He cuddles her, puts the gun back in his pocket.)*

LADY JEFFERSON LUGARD: But there is chaos – rampage. *(She looks in the direction of TRAVELER-X.)* What's that? Are we safe?

JEFFERSON LUGARD: No problem, honey. Insignificant. Just aliens crossing. We're here. The border is closed.

LADY JEFFERSON LUGARD: What? Aliens? From where? Mars? *(Looks THE TRAVELER up and down.)* Terrible specimen. What do they want?

JEFFERSON LUGARD: Entry. Illegal entry. Borders...

LADY JEFFERSON LUGARD: Cross... *(Reflecting.)* Crossing... what do they want?

JEFFERSON LUGARD: Oh, you know these people. If it's not one thing it's another. Colored... Plague. This time it's the borders. It's the borders. I think colored folks have a problem with borders if you ask me. Watch out. They're always in one border or the other. Migrating, between borders. They must like being there. Otherwise, how come they're always between borders? Colored folks like cross... Crossing... Crosses...

61

LADY JEFFERSON LUGARD: *(Drinking wine to calm herself down.)* And yet they complain?

JEFFERSON LUGARD: You mind them? They're always complaining anyway! Who listens to them? If we did, we'll never get any sleep. Them colored always full of shit... beg yea pardon...Shit! That's what they're full of. Civil Rights! Equal Opportunity and all that jazz. Well, they got it. Written of course. But who practices what's written? We interpret the law. Of course. So? You interpret it as you see it. Beauty, they say, is in the eye of the beholder. And so is the law. Not so darling? *(They laugh.)* Them colored don't know nothing about the way the system works. Otherwise, they wouldn't bother to complain about rights. To hell with them rights! Who cares! Leave them at the borders where they belong. They like it there. Colored folks love it...between... Or rather, crossing borders. Crossing waters. Crossing oceans. I know them! They'll do anything. It's in their blood. And Aliens? Another breed. They'll do anything to enter into any space. *(A crashing sound as TRAVELER-X kicks at the gate of his cell.)*

LADY JEFFERSON LUGARD: *(Scared.)* Are we safe?

JEFFERSON LUGARD: Sure are, darling. Rest.

LADY JEFFERSON LUGARD: *(Still insisting.)* Are we safe? *(The other heavenly bodies take up the chorus "Are we safe?" He kisses her, fondles her. She begins to strap her bra. He helps her do it.)*

JEFFERSON LUGARD: Go inside dear. We're secure. Dealt with it... him... No problem. Rest. I'm going on the beat. *(She exits reluctantly and he leaves.)*

TRAVELER-X: *(Screaming and pounding at the gates.)* Let me go! Let me go!

STANLEY LIVINGSTONE: You got your green card now? Do you?

TRAVELER-X: Hmm... no.

STANLEY LIVINGSTONE: Then you got no business here.

TRAVELER-X: I got business. I'm working on it.

STANLEY LIVINGSTONE: Ha! Ha! Ha! *(Mimicking him.)* "I got business. I'm working on it."

Dreamer! Slouch off. *(He moves to close Heavensgate more tightly. TRAVELER-X stretches and attempts to hold back STANLEY LIVINGSTONE's hand.)*

STANLEY LIVINGSTONE: Dare! God will strike you dead. He will. *(TRAVELER-X again makes a dash for STANLEY LIVINGSTONE's throat. STANLEY LIVINGSTONE pulls again. Fires in the air. TRAVELER-X, frustrated.)*

TRAVELER-X: My God never lies. My God never fails. Jah knows no boundaries. Jah is neither He nor She. But you, you've doctored up the spirit of God. Made God in your own image... to control. Because like everything else, you must control. Always. Heh, you guard of dishonor. Don't you change the face of my God. You won't. You don't know and never will know me, Jah. *(He blows his trumpet and sings.)* You don't know and never will know me, Jah. Jah be no man or woman. Jah be no man or woman, Me Jah is *it*! *(STANLEY LIVINGSTONE mocks and taunts him and brandishes the key.)* No, you lie! You take! Take and take! You race of takers! No one gave the keys to you! Jah never went on vacation with Peter! You stole it! You steal it. You steal to control. To own. To command. To commandeer everything. Everybody! Don't you ever tire from controlling? Space? Soul? Life? What the hell? You think you can blindfold us forever? Aren't you tired of stealing? Conquering? Raping? Don't you see you're hell? Hell on earth! What the hell are you?

THE UNSEEN: *(Voices returning in the background.)* You burn – you burn burn-burn-burn...

TRAVELER-X: And the spirits mangle (man) handle the body. Don't you tire? You think you can blindfold us, colored forever?

THE UNSEEN: You burn-you-burn-burn-burn... *(JEFFERSON LUGARD returning and walking up to take over "Freedom Wagon." He opens the front door. STANLEY LIVINGSTONE enters, JEFFERSON LUGARD on driver's seat. TRAVELER-X struggles to regain control and enters*

*"Freedom Train." They spray the chemical on TRAVEL-
ER-X who becomes temporarily demobilized. The door
is slammed in his face and he falls, dust and bruises on
his face. "Freedom Wagon" moves on. They wave him
good-bye. As they drive off, JEFFERSON LUGARD shouts
to TRAVELER-X.)*

JEFFERSON LUGARD: *(Smiling.)* Hey dreamer! Hey Martin
King's brother! How's the dream coming? Okay? Ha!
Ha! Ha! I've got a dream. I got a dream! Dream on!
Don't matter what or whether you dream. Don't care if
you're "X" spitting fire. Fighting for Freedom, Equality,
and Justice. *(Mimicking.)* "By any means possible!" La!
La! Lost Malcolm. Poor fella! Where did all that end?
Here. At the crossroads. Here Justice passes you by.
Here, Freedom Wagon is on its way again. *(Mimicking,
singing again.)* "I got a dream-I got a dream!" Equality! Freedom by any means possible. Where's that?
What country is that? What tribe's that? Hey, Heaven
is not run on quota basis. You are born into it. Birthright, ok? No quota. No gender. No color preferences in
Heaven. Heaven is serious business. Founded on solid
Justice. And I'm president. President of Heaven. I got
veto power. And I got Lincoln's pen. Hey, ride on. Ride
on Freedom Wagon! *(STANLEY LIVINGSTONE smoking
a cigar. He takes the driver's seat, ignites the motor and
turns on music. They sing as jolly fellows. A horn blasts
as they ride noisily toward the cell to taunt THE TRAV-
ELER. They nearly crush him. STANLEY LIVINGSTONE
disembarks. THE TRAVELER is rudely awakened.)*

TRAVELER-X: *(Cursing.)* Is this the land of democracy? "E
pluribus unum." Eh? One nation. One God. One des-
tiny. Is this it? *(Suddenly, siren sounds can be heard on
all sides. TRAVELER-X is almost knocked down.)*

A VOICE: *(Threatening from an ambulance.)* Give way! Give
way, you louse! *(STANLEY LIVINGSTONE acting as sheriff hurriedly appears on the scene to open Heavensgate.
A white body is wheeled to the door, but TRAVELER-X
escapes from the boundaries. Breaking through his cell.
Breaking the chains around him as he leaps forward. The*

shackles fall at the center of the crossroads as he thrusts himself forward. Loud noise echoes from his jammed cell door. SOJOURNER NKRUMAH too is awakened, up in arms and screaming. The heavenly bodies rush out in dismay. SOJOURNER NKRUMAH begins struggling to be free. But she is firmly strapped back into her place. They prepare to push in the newcomer who is still wrapped up in white shrouds.)

STANLEY LIVINGSTONE: Will you step aside?

TRAVELER-X: I WILL NOT! I was here before everyone else!

STANLEY LIVINGSTONE: Step aside or I'll shoot you!

TRAVELER-X: Go ahead! Shoot! Death is no news to a soldier. In the battlefield of life, I'm black. I've seen death. Oh, so many times. I've been dead so many times! I've been dead so many, many, many times. Death now dies in my place! What do I dare fear, when I'm already down? What do I fear? *(TRAVELER-X bangs at Heavensgate. STANLEY LIVINGSTONE is so shocked, he stands by and watches him.)*

TRAVELER-X: Open the door. Open and let me in. Ancestors, Oh Jah! Ani Earth Goddess! Onokwu Sea-River Goddess! Amadioha God of Thunder! God of Justice Amadioha! Shango! Why do you stare at me when they take my place again and push me out of the door forever? How long must I wait? How long must I wait? *(As TRAVELER-X screams, more bodies arrive at Heavensgate. The heavenly bodies are seen scrambling for safety inside Heaven. Light flashes through the transparent gates of Heaven. Pandemonium ensues. Voices of chaos and confusion inside.)*

STANLEY LIVINGSTONE: *(Frustrated, tries to resolve the problem with a scheme to distract THE TRAVELER as he pushes him.)* Now get into a single file. You can only enter Heaven in a single file, not in crowds. *(TRAVELER-X moves to the front.)*

TRAVELER-X: I was here before everyone else.

STANLEY LIVINGSTONE: *(To TRAVELER-X.)* I told you before. You need at least two forms of I.D. to get in. *(Pause.)* Your driving license?

TRAVELER-X: And I already said I have none. Let me repeat myself. How can I get a driver's license when I'm locked out... driven away? And I got no car? And I got no money? And I got no job? All I got to show is this social insecurity?

STANLEY LIVINGSTONE: No! You're wrong again! It is– Social Security.

TRAVELER-X: I know no social security. All I've seen is insecurity. All I've seen is social insecurity.

STANLEY LIVINGSTONE: *(Pushing him away.)* Sorry, I can't help you. Next! *(The newcomer wants to pass, but TRAVELER-X moves forward. The newcomer stops. Blessing TRAVELER-X.)* Rest in pieces. Better get moving now. Again, it's the hour of our housecleaning.

TRAVELER-X: What? Housecleaning? But this is Heaven!

STANLEY LIVINGSTONE: Yes? So what? Move or I'll move you!

TRAVELER-X: Justice must take its course.

STANLEY LIVINGSTONE: *(Chuckling, he pulls the railing across.)* "Watch out. Alien-crossing." Justice? *(Reinforcing the railing.)* "Watch out! Aliens-Crossing!" Ha! Ha! Ha! He's a bona fide citizen and you're not. No room for immigrants in Heaven. *(He blows the whistle and calls LADY JEFFERSON LUGARD. She appears and salutes in military fashion.)* Here. Here's a native.

LADY JEFFERSON LUGARD: What am I supposed to do with a native?

STANLEY LIVINGSTONE: Hello. Ta-ta! You kidding. To the Reservation of course. *(He yanks him. TRAVELER-X winces but stays his ground.)* Sorry, no room here. Or, you got proof of citizenship? You got a green card? A Resident Permit? Your "A" number... Alien number... You need a green card to go to Heaven. That's the law.

TRAVELER-X: I got no green card. But I got a card. I got a card, but it's black. What does it matter that any card must have a color? What should I care that any card is- is green or red or blue or brown or beige? What should I care that any card is black or white? What do I care that my card is colored?

STANLEY LIVINGSTONE: *(In the background, THE UNSEEN voices and that of SOJOURNER NKRUMAH recall the refrain, "I got a black card.")* Your card has got to be green for you to pass. No pass on red. *(Emphatically.)* No pass on red. Caution on yellow. You need the green card to life.

TRAVELER-X: I got no green card, and I must live. I got a black card, and I AM living. I got a black card, and I must live. My black card is blue sometimes, I got a black card! My black card is red sometimes, I got a black card! My black card is green sometimes, I got a black card! I got a black card that will be green some-day, Green always! What do I care now if the sign is "delayed green, " and there are flashes of red or yel-low? What do I care if there are multiple stop signs? All that I know is that I must go. And go, I must! All I know is that I must pass. I feel this right of passage! I feel this rite of passage. Since crossing the Middle Pas-sage! And pass, I must!! *(TRAVELER-X blocks the gate of Heaven with his body and begins to play a jazz tune.)*

STANLEY LIVINGSTONE: Get the hell out of here! You're causing obstruction! *(STANLEY LIVINGSTONE motions upwards. Suddenly, flashes of red light and water sprays from Heaven. LADY JEFFERSON LUGARD, descends again. This time she is even more sensuous in her lin-gerie. She puts down her bucket filled with soapy water. She swings her buttocks teasingly before TRAVELER-X. TRAVELER-X is not moved. She makes a ballet motion, spreading and revealing so much more. All this is meant to distract TRAVELER-X or to lure him away from Heav-ensgate. He's so disgusted until the woman poses as if mooning in front of him and thus further aggravating TRAVELER-X's senses. He spits.)*

TRAVELER-X: *(Scornfully.)* I thought you people were smart-er than that. How do you hope to move the spirits in me with your bottom as flat as a pan? Go check out my sistuh. Go check out my momma. *(Arrogantly in sing-song manner.)* They got dimension. Check it out! Front or back? They got dimension! Oh-so much dimension you'd get lost in the depths. So much to hold. It's so filling. So much. So much... *(At this point, STANLEY LIVINGSTONE brings out a long rope. The lady is angry and holds on to her bucket.)* Do you hope to rouse up my ancestral spirits with those bones rattling? Babe, my sistuh got drums in her thighs! My mama got music in her hips! So pack your bones out of me sight. Don't send my senses in flight. *(TRAVELER-X is still rapping and almost lost in this panegyric when suddenly, light blinks and everywhere turns red. In quick succession, STANLEY LIVINGSTONE flings the rope into a loop around TRAVELER-X's neck. He pulls away as he is screaming, while LADY JEFFERSON LUGARD pushes the waiting newcomer with the blonde hair into Heaven. The gates clang. TRAVELER-X screaming, "Help!" "Help!" "Help!" as he is being pulled away from Heavensgate while the newcomer is being smuggled into Heaven. The mission accomplished, STANLEY LIVINGSTONE releases TRAVELER-X from the leash and stands at attention before LADY JEFFERSON LUGARD who now quickly dips her hands in the bucket.)*

STANLEY LIVINGSTONE: *(In military fashion he salutes LADY JEFFERSON LUGARD.)* Mission accomplished!

LADY JEFFERSON LUGARD: *(Approving the salute in military fashion.)* All correct! Go! The souls are waiting! In his majesty's name, take! Police them!

STANLEY LIVINGSTONE: *(Salutes again.)* To the glory of she who reigns. In God we trust. *(End salute. STANLEY LIVINGSTONE departs in earnest, while Her LADY bursts into laughter.)*

LORD JEFFERSON LUGARD: *(Emerging.)* Darling, that was a great act! I'm proud of you. My Shero. Wao! Ladies and gentlemen, I present to you our new SHERO! *(They applaud. Pause.)* Any doubt still about who calls the shots here? You dig my style? Lesson one on Equal Opportunity! I said it. *(Wielding a pen.)* No Affirmative Action?

THE UNSEEN: *(Voices in the background.)* VETOED!

LORD JEFFERSON LUGARD: Justice?

THE UNSEEN: VETOED!

LORD JEFFERSON LUGARD: Freedom?

THE UNSEEN: Vetoed!

LORD JEFFERSON LUGARD: *(He opens the door of the wagon again.)* Ha! Ha! Ha! Make way! Make way! Here comes Her Majesty's "Freedom Wagon." *(Freedom wagon zooms past, splashing dust on the voices that start to choke and cough. LADY JEFFERSON LUGARD struts into Heaven. The gates are shut noisily. Lights snap. TRAVELER-X in darkness, emits an anguished cry.)*

TRAVELER-X: *(Alone.)* Jah! You are no God at all! Where God? God, where are you? I'm again played out of the game. *(Crying.)* Jah! Help! Help meee! *(Echoes of "me" bounce off and on the wall.)* Damn-it! You too, God? You too? Color blind? Eh? *(Cajoling.)* What color are you? God. Is it because you're old? Too old to make a difference? Did they put you in an old people's home as they did their momma and poppa in D.C.? God, are you a minority? A minority in heaven? You too? God? Answer me God! Where are you? Who are you, Jah? *(Mood changes to a wooing, courtship dance. Slow, soothing melody in the background.)* Ha! Jah, you're a woman! Yea God, I know. You're a woman. *(He pushes his chest out, strutting and mimicking ladies in heels.)* Bragging, eh? Hey, come on babe. We can work it out- can work it out. We gonna work it out-can work it out! You see, Jah. *(He struts up and down still like a lady.)* See? See? See? I got sex appeal. *(He does a sensuous dance step. At this point, angry voices rise in the background and in TRAVELER-X's eye, he can see and feel fingers taunting and poking him with pain. He becomes delirious.)* Okay! Okay! Okay! Stop! For God's sake, stop! God, Forgive. In the name of Jah, forgive. Forgive my mouth. *(Scream-*

ing.) Yes, I know. Yes, I know. Jah, you're a man! You got muscle! I see. See your muscle, God. *(More angry voices in the background and fingers poking TRAVELER-X as he runs around and around.)* Oh! Jah! Where did I go wrong again? Jah, where do I go from here? I'm damned forward or backward! *(More fingers poking and their voices rising in anger.)* Stop! Stop this, God! Stop! If this is a joke, stop! Stop it, God! *(More torment for TRAVELER-X.)* I'm done! No use trying. Forward or backward I lose again, God! Where's your measure? *(More angry voices like swarming flies and fingers poking pain into his entire being. TRAVELER-X's face is scarified by the fingers of flame. His growing pain leads him deeper into delirium until totally overwhelmed, he tears his agbada to cover up some of the gaping wounds. But the taunting continues as he struggles and with a note of finality, yells and throws himself on the ground and passes out. His drum, trumpet and other possessions are scattered on the ground as he lies there and begins to dream about Idu, his mythical homeland in Africa. As he passes out, light snaps to total blackout for a brief moment.)*

END PASSAGE: The Dream Sequence

(TRAVELER-X lies in a Twilight Zone. Time is just before dawn and THE TRAVELER sees himself in the ritual before homecoming. He is trekking along the Route XYZ with a certain measure of urgency until he enters the outskirts of Idu. In the distance, he hears the sound of drums, xylophones, flutes, udu (a clay pot with a double tongue), isiaka (rattle beads), akpele (horn from antelope), and a host of other traditional instruments that confirm and chorus the collective voices of this community. But put together, the voices are muffled and even though TRAVELER-X is much closer to the sounds, they sound faint, feeble until overtaken by the Agogo- a metal gong and the mask and voice of GRIOT, the town crier who looks like him, his other self in the other world. He gets confused as the new face meets this old face that looks so young and yet so ancient. He touches his many faces/masks and screams in fear of his multiple personality: one mask as FATHER GRIOT, another as TRAVELER-X, and the other as GARVEY MANDELA. In this dream, TRAVELER-X has a red mask and a three-piece suit. Inside, he wears his tattered agbada, and he has lost his drums.)

THE MASK OF TRAVELER-X AS GRIOT: *(Beats his gong three times.)* Idu, it's yet another season! The yam stakes have lost their girdles! In spite of the seasons of drought, earth still swells. Yielding her bowels for us to feed. Idu! It's yet another season of passage. Gather the yams! Roast them together! Cart away the dirt of seasons passing. Eat the yams together, that we may yet witness another season, together... *(Even before the GRIOT has completed his rounds, his words have been overtaken by the noisy rhythm of rap-music coming from a jukebox. Teenagers gather and watch. One teenage girl possessed in a new dance. Youths to be played*

71

by THE UNSEEN. TRAVELER-X watches in dismay. He stands behind a nearby tree. He can see SOJOURNER NKRUMAH very faintly, now acting the role of his mother. And his other self, GARVEY MANDELA, looking like THE FATHER. They all center themselves in front of the ancestral grotto to commence the rites of passage. SO-JOURNER NKRUMAH as THE MOTHER carries a bundle of firewood, which she hurriedly puts together while the mask of GARVEY MANDELA puts the yam tuber at the center of the fire, pours libation onto the earth and begins her invocations to the ancestors. THE MOTH-ER/SOJOURNER NKRUMAH is still struggling, fanning frantically to get the wood to catch fire and roast the yam. The youths continue their dance, oblivious to the urgency of the ritual around them, until SOJOURNER NKRUMAH blossoms fully into THE MOTHER. She is an enraged mother, screaming at her daughter.)

THE MOTHER: *(Blowing the fire.)* Winnie! *(No answer.)* Idia! *(No answer.)* Sojourner! *(No answer.)* Stop that dance of death and come over here to help a tired woman! *(The youth continue their dance. Then the mask of GARVEY MANDELA as THE FATHER rises from the bellows and moves directly to the jukebox, grabs it and smashes it to the ground, thus halting the youths and the music. He now takes up his bellows as if to blow life into the dying fire. WINNIE IDIA as THE DAUGHTER is now forced to listen to the old mother as SOJOURNER NKRUMAH makes one final attempt at blowing the fire. Wiping the sweat from her brow and giving up.)* Now you blow this too! I've been trying for so many seasons to light this fire. Blow it. It's your turn, now! But instead, you go on dancing naked. Feasting eyes while the smoke consumes the yam grown from seasons of flooding the earth with our blood. *(THE DAUGHTER bends down to blow the fire but it is just too hard.)* Tell me how this family will eat the New Yam with the rest of the world if our lungs are too weak to blow the fire that will roast the yam? *(TOWNCRIER's gong is heard. THE MOTHER/ SOJOURNER NKRUMAH, panicking.)* Blow the fire hard! Hard! Hear the crier! We have just one more chance to eat the new yam. Blow the fire now!

THE DAUGHTER: *(Struggling, giving up and protesting.)* Blame the youth! Blame! Blame us- Blame the youth. As if we caused the rains. Has it not been raining? Long? Hasn't it been raining long, long before we were born? And haven't you refused to hear me, when I tell you that firewood is out of fashion?

THE MOTHER: *(Sarcastically.)* "Generation-X, now the Dot. com kids." I heard the teacher call you people the other day. I still don't-can't understand what that means even after he explained it to us. I still don't. Can't understand the youth of today. They beat my imagination! Children from a strange world. Firewood is out of fashion, eh? Why can't you attract a suitor with money to wipe the sweat from my brow? Ehn? Day in day out, all you do is dance and dream of a no-no land. Neverland. Amilika! Gamany! Falanci! All those lands where people fly to heaven with their wings! It's the dream that took your brother. Then he was Martin X. Yesterday he became Nkrumah, then Garvey, and then Mandela. Who knows what he's become now? Who knows? It's the fat dream that took him to Amilika. For seasons we've been waiting for his promises. Promises... Promises... Are we going to eat promises? We have children so that our world will be better. We have children so that their world will be better than ours. *(THE FATHER who has been silent now rises.)*

THE FATHER: *(Scornfully.)* Now you two, stop your noise! You complain and complain like flies quarreling over lack of water in the dry season. Why blame this daughter as if she caused the rain? When your son who left this land long ago to bring us the new life, stays there, relishing his wealth and doesn't care if we die or live? Just leave the girl alone. Leave the youth alone to her new dance, if that will drown her tears! We need laughter to survive in this world. Leave the girl to dance...

THE MOTHER: Her chance of death! She must know we're in this mess together. And if she must, she must learn the art of holding back tears like I've done for so many seasons.

THE FATHER: Go on complaining! It's all you women know. Soon, the crier will sound the final note and this family will have no yam to present and celebrate the new season! *(The final note of the drum voices. THE MOTHER in panic, bends by the fire and starts poking it together with THE FATHER and THE DAUGHTER. The whole family struggles with the fire as the sounds of drum swell the air to mark the eating of the New Yam as the beginning of the New Year.)*

THE MOTHER: *(Pushing THE DAUGHTER to dance.)* Go! Go and dance on our behalf.

THE DAUGHTER: *(Resisting.)* But the yam is not done.

THE FATHER: *(Impatiently scraping the yam.)* Dance! Dance! Let's not be left out of the season! *(THE MOTHER moves towards THE DAUGHTER, takes up her hand and begins to show her an ancient dance step. THE DAUGHTER tries to imitate her when THE FATHER, who has been trying to scrape the bark off the half-roasted yam, drops it with the result that it breaks into so many pieces. He crosses the pieces of yam, goes over to THE MOTHER to join the ancient dance step, when suddenly, TRAVELER-X as GARVEY MANDELA's double mask, emerges and joins in the ritual dance. This brings a new energy and excitement into the scene.)*

THE MOTHER: *(Excitedly pushing THE DAUGHTER to dance with the stranger.)* At last, night is over! The Gods have heard our voices! Dance with him! Here's the new man we've been waiting for! Here's your man, Amilika! Amilika is Heaven! His voice will light the fire! His voice will quench the smoke of seasons, blinding our sight.

THE FATHER: Dance! Let him not dance yet. He must be tired after traveling such a great distance. Let him rest first. Then he'll mark the new season with us. *(THE FATHER runs his fingers down the velveteen sheen of THE TRAVELER's three-piece suit with extreme admiration. Adoring the stranger and turning to his wife.)* Hmm. What the children of this generation can do! I tell you, the days are gone when we lived in darkness.

We walked on our feet. But the children of today have no use for legs. They fly in the sky across the ocean because they have wings.

THE MOTHER: *(Takes up THE TRAVELER's hand as if showing him off to the world.)* Turn around. He's so much like our son. Turn... *(TRAVELER-X turns around.)* Oh, God you are here at last! Up there, where you're inside that big bird – "alupileni." *Do you sit on your back or with your bottom as we do? (THE TRAVELER, still as the twin or double mask of GARVEY MANDELA chuckles again.)* You laugh, our newcomer. Forgive our ignorance. Our generation is blind as a bat. But we long to see beyond. We long to know. *(Pause.)* So now, tell us you who see God in the New World - What is the face of God like? What color is God? Do you think God sees our suffering? Does God know that it's been raining here for several seasons? Following a very long season of drought? And now it's the New Yam festival. See how small our yams are? Does God know that the land is flooded with tears? And the wood no longer burns to roast our yams? *(THE TRAVELER's twin or double chuckles again.)*

THE FATHER: Tell me, how's the face of God? What color is God? In the New World, is God black or white?

THE MOTHER: How could you be asking such questions? Isn't it obvious? God certainly can't bear your color or mine. God is white. God must be white! Don't you see it? The altar? His white hands spread across? His hair hanging loose like corn tassels on his shoulders? Don't you see our women nowadays fry their hair and scrape their skin with soap to look like him?

THE FATHER: Is it only the women? I've also seen our men fry and roll their hair and I tell you, they look quite gay to me!

THE MOTHER: They looked to me more like wet chickens in the rain. I've seen black women color their eyes blue.

THE FATHER: *(To the masks of THE TRAVELER.)* Ha! Ha! Ha! That must be the fashion in Heaven. Is it not? *(THE TRAVELER is beginning to lose his patience. He doesn't chuckle anymore, he grins.)* Forgive us great one if we seem to be asking too many questions. We have to rely on the words of a stranger to shape our truths. You see, our son, too, is in Amilika. But he won't tell us anything. He's drinking tea in the New World and has forgotten us. Our son has forgotten us. You must have seen my son riding in those long, long cars. Tell me, great stranger from Amilika - Did you see my son? *(Silence.)* He left us long ago. He left us... crossed to... to Amilika. *(Pause.)* Ah... Amilika! Where they all go and never return! Amilika! Where they take and take and never give back in return! Did you see my son? Did you see him on the road? Is he coming? Will he come...?

THE MOTHER: To open the door for us.

THE FATHER: We're still waiting for passports. Son. I know you'll be returning soon, I know. It's too humid here, son. You'll be returning soon. But stranger, son... ehm... please, when you see my son, tell him that we're still waiting.

THE MOTHER: Tell him we've waited for seasons for him to open that gateway for us. *(Calling.)* Daughter! *(Silence.)* Winnie! *(Silence.)* Idia!

THE DAUGHTER: *(Responding.)* Here, Mother!

THE MOTHER: *(Handing over the bowl containing an item of sacrifice to THE DAUGHTER.)* Take this to the cross-roads! *(THE DAUGHTER runs to perform the ritual at the crossroads.)*

THE DAUGHTER: Uke! You trickster spirit at the crossroads. Eat. Eshu! Legba! Elegbara! Eat!! And you, unsmiling spirits, eat and leave us our road. We have waited long enough. *(THE DAUGHTER returns, panting. Concurrently, drums and flutes, trumpets and xylophones rise from the background. THE DAUGHTER begins to dance. THE MOTHER and THE FATHER also dance. THE TRAVELER joins in the dance, facing THE DAUGHTER. The atmosphere is gleeful until the dance/music reaches a climax and everyone appears so possessed by joy when suddenly, THE TRAVELER pulls off the mask, revealing his true identity. He also pulls off his three-piece suit and jerri-curled wig to show the tattered agbada covering him. The atmosphere is now tense. The people recognize him, but they are also stunned and shocked by this revelation that they all retreat from him. THE DAUGHTER runs out of sight. THE FATHER, seeming to have recovered from his shock, screams.)*

THE FATHER: Garvey...Mandela? *(Echoes of "GARVEY... MANDELA" fill the air and they run to him.)*

THE MOTHER: My son? *(Silence.)*

THE FATHER: My son? *(Silence.)*

THE MOTHER: *(Disengaging from him after staring at him for a while.)* No! You can't be my son! No! You Gods! Ancestors! Come and see what beast has risen from the New World! *(Silence.)* Swear that you are my son!!

TRAVELER-X: Mama, I'm your son, Garvey... Mandela.

THE FATHER: No! You can't be my son! My son is in Amilika.

THE MOTHER: My son can't be in rags! My son can't be without shoes like us here.

THE FATHER: Get the hell out of here or else I will sound the drums of war! And soon the entire world will be here to lynch you. How on earth can you be faking the ghost of my son who is so much alive?

THE MOTHER: Perhaps he is a witch. We must be ready to kill this harmful spirit. *(THE MOTHER is about to strike but THE FATHER intervenes.)*

THE FATHER: Don't strike it, I say. He's just an ill-fated ghost. Dead men don't bite. But if he pretends to be our son...

TRAVELER-X: What do you think I'll gain by faking to be your son? How can you be so blind, you no longer know your son? *(Showing the tattoos on his chest.)* Here. Here. If you still doubt me, are these not the tattoos you made on my chest at my naming? *(Turning his back.)* Is this not the scar left from the wounds I sustained when I fell from the palm tree while tapping

77

palm wine? How then can you now doubt that I am your son at my homecoming? *(Silence. UNSEEN VOICES offstage follow with echoes of "Homecoming, Homecoming, Homecoming!")*

THE FATHER: Hmm... It is not that we doubt. But that our son should return to us in tattered clothes after so many years in God's own land? Amilika they say is heaven. God's own country. *(Pause.)* Where's the milk and honey you brought for us? How can you return to us with your hands empty? How? After so many years of being in Heaven, how do you fall back like this into our Hell? What happened to the dream? Where is our share of the dream?

TRAVELER-X: *(Presenting his other faces.)* Father! There was no dream. Never was a dream. It's all been a myth. Myths created by those who command the word to mystify us. *(Silence.)* Mama, America's no heaven. America Is a Soap Bubble.

THE FATHER: No! Not Amilika! God's own country...

TRAVELER-X: *(Enraged.)* Run by the devil! *(Silence.)*

THE MOTHER: Hmm! You are crazy! How can you say such a forbidden thing?

TRAVELER-X: America is no Heaven, mother.

THE MOTHER and THE FATHER: Stop! You heretic. You are blaspheming! Sh! Sh! Sh! Stop before they crucify you. Walls have ears, you know. *(They look around to see if anyone else is listening.)*

TRAVELER-X: Yes! America is nothing. If anything, it's an empty shell. Or at best, hell on earth.

THE FATHER: You lie! You wretched thing! How can you say such forbidden things? When your mates go there in a blink of an eye, they already flood their homes with gold and silver. And crack up the roads with long, long cars: *(Counting.)* 4 x 4, Patufainda, Babemacedez, Leg-size, Mazida, Folifo, Tayuta, five-o-four, "five-o-ten?" So where were you when others sent home their booties? If Amilika's no Heaven, how, my son, do they get these things?

TRAVELER-X: Trafficking.

THE FATHER: Trafficking on what?

TRAVELER-X: On human soul. Body. Everything!

THE FATHER: *(Spitefully.)* Hmm... Go and sit down!

THE MOTHER: Or better still, get lost!

THE FATHER: You are nothing but a failure.

THE MOTHER: *(Crying.)* Why will my things always be so different? When others go, the road is clear. When it's my turn, the roads cross each other. And I stand trapped at the crossroads. When will my dream of Heaven ever come? When? *(Dismissing him.)* Just go! Go! And don't open my wounds afresh!

THE FATHER: *(Chewing his tobacco.)* You are nothing but a failure. Just get out of my sight!

TRAVELER-X: *(Passionately.)* How can you reject me? Why should I be rejected? Again, rejected for the countless time? Can't you see my clothes are torn? Can't you see my clothes are worn? For endless seasons, I've been toiling. I've been failing, for seasons. I've been searching and searching. Been tested and tested for thousands of jobs. Been so close. So many times to enter the gates of Heaven. But each time, every time, I've been rejected. Rejected. Rejected. I've got a thousand letters to prove it – *(THE UNSEEN voices take up the refrain "Rejected, Rejected, Always Rejected" as TRAVELER-X pulls out a letter from his pocket and reads:)*

Dear Mr. X:

This is to thank you for your great interest in applying for the position of Deputy Associate Assistant Janitor with our establishment. There were numerous applicants with highly competitive credentials. There were many exceptional candidates who qualified for the position. I regret to inform you, however, that after reviewing your application, you failed to meet our criteria for appointment. Please, accept our gratitude for the interest you have shown with our establishment. We wish you luck in your search.

Yours truly,
Chair of Heaven.

(Silence.) This is it. This is what my life has been. Searching. Searching. Wandering. Trying and failing so many times. I do not fail for lack of trying.

THE FATHER: *(Parodying him.)* I do not fail for lack of trying. So why do you fail? Why do you fail, where others succeed?

TRAVELER-X: Because I don't have the right card!

THE MOTHER: The right card? What do you mean? Amilika is heaven. That is my understanding. Does anyone need any card to enter Heaven?

TRAVELER-X: Does anyone have to die to go to Heaven? Ask me. *(They stare at him.)* Ask me. Can you enter Heaven without dying? *(Silence.)* Now you can see, mother and father. It costs more to die than to live. It costs more to die than to live. And you need not only have the card with the right color, but a visa too! Yes, a visa! I've spent all my life trying, until I could go no more. The system took my soul and I died!

THE MOTHER and THE FATHER: You did what?

TRAVELER-X: I died!

THE FATHER: You died? In Heaven?

TRAVELER-X: Yes, I died.

THE FATHER: So, if you died... How come you're here now?

TRAVELER-X: I was rejected. The gates were locked.

THE MOTHER: *(Hysterical.)* Does anyone else die in Heaven? You people of the world hear me? Answer me? Does anyone else die in Heaven? Everyone goes to Heaven to live. My son goes to Heaven to die!! *(Running amuck to the village.)* Winnie! Idia! Sojourner! Nkrumah! Come! Come. Hear the word for this season! It is only we who go to Heaven to die! *(She returns to the scene. Pause.)*

TRAVELER-X: Believe me, I've tried. I've tried. But life is hard. Life is hard, Mother. I've tried so hard to find life and match it with justice. Life's so hard, but justice is harder to find.

THE FATHER: Well, continue to find it then! Is it me you hope will find it in my old age? My time is already gone. We may have been here these long seasons, our generation has no strength left. But you are young. You got the power. And you can speak the language of the new world. Go back! Bear down your weight until the gates give way to your command. Return! Go open the door! We will join you, soon! Go in peace! *(TRAVELER-X turns to go. THE MOTHER begins incantations as she sprinkles white clay.)*

THE MOTHER: Ancestors! Guide the feet of the traveling one. May he never stumble on the crossroads! *(She does her ritual again.)* Uke! Eshu! Elegba! Iegba! Eat and let him pass! Let the traveler name his passage.

THE UNSEEN: *(Returning.)* Traveler! Traveler! Traveler! Name your passage! Name your passage! Traveler! Traveler! Traveler! Name your passage! Name your passage! *(At this point, siren sound is heard. TRAVELER-X is startled and springs to his feet. He is now fully awake.)*

TRAVELER-X: *(Reflecting.)* So, I have been dreaming? Yes, I've been dreaming *(Staring. Pause.)* Hmn, but...but I got the vision. I see the road. I see... *(Another bout of sirens sound. STANLEY LIVINGSTONE is in the near distance. Lights are flashing and it is again obvious that they are rolling another newcomer into Heaven. TRAVELER-X adjusts himself and takes a firm position at Heavensgate. Sirens blow. Cars honking as in a traffic jam. STANLEY LIVINGSTONE shouts at TRAVELER-X to clear from the gate, but TRAVELER-X is defiant. SOJOURNER NKRUMAH is fully awake. She starts singing the gospel song, "Steal, Steal Away to Jesus, I got no long time to stay here." Exasperated, the gatekeepers seize her and put additional reinforcements in her cell.)*

STANLEY LIVINGSTONE: Give way! *(Silence.)* Out of the way! We have a VIP! *(Silence.)* Give way, dummy! *(JEFFERSON LUGARD enters with "Freedom Wagon." TRAVELER-X is still in the way. The gatekeepers blasts the horn. Rides recklessly to crush TRAVELER-X. TRAVELER-X jumps, staggers. SOJOURNER NKRUMAH holds him to keep him from falling. STANLEY LIVINGSTONE thrusts his baton forward to strike TRAVELER-X's head, but THE TRAVEL-ER seizes the baton from STANLEY LIVINGSTONE and strikes him on the head, while SOJOURNER NKRUMAH pushes JEFFERSON LUGARD out of the "Freedom Wagon." Then TRAVELER-X helps to take off her shackles as she intensifies her struggle. They jump in and cruise away with ferocious speed, leaving a dense fog of smoke behind them.)*

TRAVELER-X: *(Jeering.)* Your mother! *(STANLEY LIVING-STONE swoons, falling to the ground. The glass doors of Heavensgate crash open, waking up the newcomer. Heaven is now left bare. The inhabitants in disarray and running away to the innermost corner as SOJOURNER NKRUMAH and TRAVELER-X search STANLEY LIV-INGSTONE and seize the keys to Heaven. Immediate-ly, TRAVELER-X takes position at the gates of Heaven. The newcomer is still trying to attain full wakefulness from his death. LORD JEFFERSON LUGARD falls and is with STANLEY LIVINGSTONE. SOJOURNER NKRUMAH jumps into his lap, while THE TRAVELER picks up the gun, flings and plays with the keys. When LORD JEF-FERSON LUGARD rises fully, he takes a step to come in, but TRAVELER-X bars the gates.)*

TRAVELER-X: You cannot pass. I got the keys! *(LORD JEF-FERSON LUGARD looks at the face of obstruction, rec-ognizes it to be TRAVELER-X.)*

JEFFERSON LUGARD: *(Alarmed.)* My God! My slave? You? Zik...ehm...Garvey Mandela...X? Goodness! Heavens! God, where are you? *(LORD JEFFERSON LUGARD faints. Music and neon lights rise from Zero Exit – Hell. SOJOURNER NKRUMAH now dressed as a disc-jockey, struts, crosses over to Hellsgate and back to Heaven. In a southern accent, she shouts.)*

SOJOURNER NKRUMAH: Yeah! The border is open - Yo'll come! Come on! Ride! Ride "Freedom Train." It bees dat way. Sometimes. Come on! Ida! Momma! Poppa!

Uncle Charlie! Winnie! Idia! Movemi! Fatima! Wangari! Ify! Nwa Odiwe! Yo'll in the hood. "Freedom Train" is here. Yeah, Soul Train. Ride! Ride "Freedom Train!" It's where the action is! The wind is on, and the world goes round! Ride! Ride! Ride "Freedom Train!" *(One by one, they gather and jump into Heaven, into "Freedom Train.")* Freeway! Free ticket! Free parking! No passport, No visa. Ride! Ride! Ride "Freedom Train." This is our land. Ride! *(JEFFERSON LUGARD, trying to rise, staggers and falls on STANLEY LIVINGSTONE, waking him up in the process. They stagger like people who are drunk. STANLEY LIVINGSTONE tries to steady himself and help JEFFERSON LUGARD who is staggering and falling. They both fall down again. "Freedom Train" whistles and moves on. They are still at Heavensgate.)*

SOJOURNER NKRUMAH: *(As disc jockey.)* You can't stop this train, Mister! This is MY "Freedom Train!" Don't you dare lay your hand on our wagon. Our "Freedom Train." Take your time. Hey! No worry! No hurry! *(SOJOURNER NKRUMAH crosses over and kisses TRAVELER-X at Heavensgate. THE UNSEEN return.)*

SOJOURNER NKRUMAH: Is everyone ready? Yeah! Garvey! Griot! Mandela! Malcolm! Martin! Momma! Poppa! Let's go! *(Chanting amidst drumming, dancing and music.)*

THE UNSEEN: Welcome! Welcome! Welcome! Welcome, brother! Welcome, sistuh! Welcome! *(The chorus rises.)* Go down Moses. Go down to Egypt land. *(Repeat the song here.)* And tell ole Pharaoh let my people go!

(As the voices are ending, SOJOURNER NKRUMAH raises another familiar tune. TRAVELER-X joins her and they do a duet until TRAVELER-X overtakes the moment with a jazz tune. STANLEY LIVINGSTONE and JEFFERSON LUGARD stand by a corner while the heavenly bodies, LADY JEFFERSON LUGARD and the previous newcomer to Heaven stand by in utter admiration and disbelief. It is obvious as they shake their heads that they do enjoy the music. Once TRAVELER-X has ended his tune, he

stares in their direction while SOJOURNER NKRUMAH glares at JEFFERSON LUGARD and STANLEY LIVING-STONE. TRAVELER-X swings the keys to Heavensgate. The heavenly bodies become bashful and retreat to a corner while TRAVELER-X and SOJOURNER NKRUMAH make their advancement into Heaven. The inhabitants of Heaven retreat while TRAVELER-X and SOJOURNER NKRUMAH advance further. STANLEY LIVINGSTONE and JEFFERSON LUGARD stupefied and restless at Heavensgate. TRAVELER-X slams the gate after them and walks towards the throne. The heavenly bodies frightened, scream. TRAVELER-X tries to sit. He falls down. SOJOURNER NKRUMAH laughs and joins him. They lie as if making love to each other amidst the pandemonium of the heavens, scandalized. Blackout. Yet the music plays on.)

ABOUT THE AUTHOR

Author of many award winning plays, Tess Onwueme has earned international acclaim as one of Africa's finest women writers. She earned her PhD from the University of Benin, Nigeria in 1987, following her Master's and Bachelor's degrees from the University of Ife, Nigeria in 1982 and 1979, respectively. After years of teaching in both American and Nigerian universities, in 1994 Dr. Onwueme was appointed Distinguished Professor of Cultural Diversity and Professor of English at the University of Wisconsin, Eau Claire, Wisconsin where she still teaches to date.

Her creative works include: *No Vacancy* (2005), *What Mama Said* (2003), *Then She Said it* (2002), *Shakara: Dance Hall Queen* (2000), *Tell it to Women* (1997), *The Missing Face* (1997), *Three Plays* (1993), *Legacies* (1989), *The Reign of Wazobia* (1988), *Mirror for Campus* (1987), *Ban Empty Barn and Other Plays* (1986), *The Desert Encroaches* (1985), *The Broken Calabash* (1984), *A Hen Too Soon* (1983), and the novel, *Why The Elephant Has No Butt* (2000).

Dr. Onwueme was born in Ogwashi-Uku, Delta State, Nigeria. She is married with five children: Kenolisa Onwueme, Ebele Onwueme, Kunume Onwueme, Bundo Onwueme, and Malije Onwueme.